To Sue

With my best wishes

No More Leaning on Lamp-Posts

Managing Uncertainty the Nick Charles Way

[signature]

Ian

No More Leaning on Lamp-Posts

Managing Uncertainty the Nick Charles Way

Ian Angell

VILLA PUBLISHING

Published 2005 by Villa Publishing Ltd.
Reg. No. 5431109
Victoria Road, Diss, Norfolk IP22 4JG

ISBN 1-902573-07-2

A CIP catalogue record for this book is available from
the British Library.

Cover Design © Ian and Mary Angell 2005
Printed and bound in Great Britain by
Creative Print and Design (Wales) Ebbw Vale

1 2 3 4 5 6 7 8 9

Contents

Dedication

This book is dedicated to the myriad victims of management methods churned out by so-called business experts. It was written for the legion of employees, shareholders, suppliers and customers who have suffered at the hands of second-rate managers - managers who choose to rely on the nonsense simply because they lack the ability to make their own decisions.

Apart from these sufferers, the book is also dedicated to all those sensible managers who, although doubting the latest trendy garbage, are obliged to implement it. They know full well that each new method will have a half-life of at most five years - the mean time it takes for the limitations to be inevitably found out and the method discarded. For every method assumes the world is black and white, whereas business operates in grey areas. Managers, particularly those running small and medium sized enterprises (SMEs), must stop hiding behind methods, and take responsibility for their own actions - after all, that is what they are paid for!

This book was written as a reality check. It is the story of Nick Charles, a businessman who says the 'how' of business must come from 'knowing' what to do, and not from the by-product of some bland generic process. Method is fine for dealing with tidy administrative issues and conforming to regulations, but is useless when it comes to making deals and chasing profits. Just how useless we shall see in Nick's business dealings in a very untidy world of risk and uncertainty. "In the world where I operate, method is the first, the last, in fact the only resort of the mediocre."

Acknowledgements

I am particularly indebted to Nick Charles, Kelly Miller, Teresa Weiler, Nikki de Villiers, and Daniel Tarrant. Nick and Kelly, of course, for sparing the time to share their stories with me, and without whom there would be no book; Teresa for supplying huge amounts of supporting material, and for her microscopic checking of the details; Nikki for running Chaucer Clinic when all this talking was going on; and Daniel for his painstaking work on the book's design and presentation.

Then there are my good friends Pat Crimmin, Neil Gregory, Rachel Hanig, and Ashutosh Khanna who gave freely of their time to read and re-read the text, and who gave me such very useful comments.

I would also like to express my gratitude to the Engineering and Physical Sciences Research Council as the initial research, prior to me writing this book, was undertaken as part of EPSRC project GR/R37753 at the London School of Economics: 'Enabling the Integration of Diverse Socio-cultural and Technical Systems within a Turbulent Social Ecosystem', and funded under the Systems Integration Initiative.

Preface

The Professor and the Tramp

"Why would a professor be interested in a drunk, and want to write a book about him?" I frequently get asked that question by both my colleagues and students at the London School of Economics. It's not really surprising since I do have a most unlikely friendship with the drunk in question, Nick Charles - the teetotal professor and the tramp! Nick, of course, is an ex-drunk, and he has been on the wagon for three decades. Nick himself has asked me many, many times why I wanted to write this book. He is genuinely baffled that I find him, and what he does, fascinating. Nick is equally perplexed when I introduce him to groups of my graduate students, from all corners of the globe, and they sit entranced as he regales them with stories of his life as an entrepreneur. It is these students who convinced me that I should write this book.

Nick Charles has always been a 'wheeler-dealer,' from his school-days (he left school aged fifteen,) through his time as a down-and-out on London's streets, to the founding and running of Chaucer Clinic, Britain's largest private clinic for alcoholics. His is an inspiring tale of what he learned as a 'dosser,' and how he uses those lessons managing and raising funds for the Clinic. This was entrepreneurship in the raw; management like I'd never seen it before.

If we hadn't been neighbours, I would never have met Nick, and never heard how he used to own a string of nearly thirty ladies hair salons. How he sang on the Northern Club circuit; and ran his own circuit of entertainers, supplying acts to two and a half thousand pubs and hotels in the South-East. How he was a boxing promoter, a theatre publicist, a personal publicist, a magazine owner, and a manager of a string of 'glamour models' and 'strippers.' Nick owns his own publishing company, and has an option on the rights to a cable TV channel; not forgetting the very risky business of running a clinic for alcoholics! He has made, and lost, millions (almost all of the losses from subsidising his work with alcoholics.)

Nick started each of his businesses with nothing, and I really mean nothing - not for him daddy's money underwriting a self-indulgent son's hobby. Each time he walked away from a business (for a variety of reasons), he would have to start all over again - usually with nothing. Nothing, that is, other than the support of the group of friends that he has made along the way, and who happily get involved with each new venture for the sheer fun and excitement of it. Nick is an original - an archetypal risk-taker with the knack of motivating everyone who works for him, and with him. "Why would a professor be interested in writing a book about Nick Charles?" How could this professor not be interested?

My students are fascinated by entrepreneurship, and are forever inquiring into the skills necessary for a successful entrepreneur - no doubt many intend to go on and make their own personal fortunes after completing their studies. When they asked about the management literature on entrepreneurship, I would direct them, but with little enthusiasm, to the sanitised 'autobiographies' of successful businessmen and women, and toward various 'how to' books - in other words, to the 'usual suspects.'

Some years ago, in a weak moment during one particular seminar, and for some light relief, I happened to mention that I knew an entrepreneur with some very radical views about running small and medium sized enterprises: my friend and neighbour, Nick Charles. His story immediately caught the students' imagination, and they badgered me for more and more information about him. Consequently, I approached Nick and asked for his help in writing a lecture that would recount his management style. I had mentioned Nick because at the time I was undertaking research into 'complexity and uncertainty in turbulent social ecosystems,' and since his business life is nothing if not turbulent, I had asked Nick's consent to him being a case study. Somewhat bemused (and amused), he agreed. As our discussions progressed I soon realised that there was far too much material to fit into a mere one-hour lecture slot, or even one case study report. Furthermore, interviews with Nick (and his wife Kelly) became almost surreal, and it soon became clear to me that the normal academic mode of publication for this study was totally inappropriate, and a far more radical and multi-layered approach was called for. What is more, I sensed that my findings would have a more general appeal. Hence the idea gradually occurred to me of writing a book, aimed at a wider public, about this exceptional man. For Nick Charles is a truly exceptional man - just how exceptional should become clear very quickly.

As I set about recounting his insights and their development, my text took on a form less and less like an academic paper, or even a business book, and instead began to coalesce around my telling of Nick's life story. I spent many laughter-packed hours finding out about his business dealings. Each time I raised a particular issue on complexity and uncertainty in management with him, Nick would illustrate his thinking on the topic with a tale about his highly colourful (mis)adventures that read more like fiction than fact. I would ask him an academic/management-type question and then sit back to tape-record his responses. However, these interviews would inevitably veer off on a random walk, only tenuously linked to whatever issue that started the discussion.

Naturally I needed to lay out the narrative of our conversations in some kind of order, although not necessarily in the sequence of the interviews. It didn't take long for me to realise that the final structure of the book was staring me in the face! I would report Nick's anecdotal answers more or less chronologically, mapping out his life story. As for the writing style, because my dialogues with Nick (more often his monologues) made such a deep impression on me, I decided to reflect those personal impressions - hence my (some would say excessive) use of 'I', the first personal singular, in the text, and for which I make no apology.

I also make liberal use of Nick's quotations gleaned from my interviews with him, although I will admit to the artistic licence of putting some of my own words into his mouth, when the situation called for bringing certain business issues to the surface - for that too I make no apology. And as for the end-product: what started out as a research case study, ended up as an account of my personal reaction to conversations about his life-story. I found

myself writing a biography aimed at a much more general reader-
ship, one that enjoys learning about the exploits of larger-than-life
characters.

Be clear, this is NOT a 'how to' book. No! This is a life-story - the
life-story of a DRUNK. For Nick was a drunk. I am not just talking
here about the odd legless social embarrassment of losing control
after drinking to excess. Nick was your classic down-and-out
alcoholic tramp - a genuine facedown in the gutter, stinking of
vomit, excrement and urine, drunken bum. After one protracted
'detox' in the psychiatric/alcoholic ward of the then St. Leonard's
hospital in Dalston, and before being let loose on an unsuspecting
world again, a nurse brought a sober Nick a disgusting collection
of clothes. "I'm not putting those on," he said. "Well you took them
off," came the accusing reply. The filthy rags were assigned to the
incinerator. With his clothes now ashes, a very generous Salvation
Army officer loaned him some clothes - the alternative was a stark
naked Nick walking the streets. He left St. Leonard's, holding a
Bible and with the apparent rank of Captain in the 'Sally Army,'
determined, as usual, never to return. That determination rarely
lasted out the week.

Ultimately, however, during one such lapse back into sobriety, a
sense of shame at his degradation forced Nick to reassess his life,
and through sheer bloody-mindedness he managed to pull
himself back from the brink, before setting out on his life's journey
to help other hopeless alcoholics. His approach is the only real
alternative to Alcoholics Anonymous for the many drunks who
want to sort out their lives, but for whom, like Nick, the 'Twelve
Steps of AA' have failed. Through his work at Chaucer, Nick
became the first ever person to be honoured "for services to
people with alcohol problems" with an MBE in the 1996 New
Year's Honours List.

Nick is no run-of-the-mill small businessman. Consequently this
book does not contain the usual simplistic, patronising (and
ultimately futile) solutions that many business books recommend
to the despairing businessman and woman in their quest to escape
the vicious circle of stress that is their everyday experience of
business decision-making. "There are no solutions, only decisions.
And a decision must be seen as the start of a new journey, rather
than the end of an old one."

The book is not a prescription for dealing with everyday life either - "as if there is a difference?" What follows is the narrative description of one drunk's personal management education, accumulated on his private journey to hell and back. It is left to the readers to take from this book what they will. Those who are not interested in the management sections can just skip them, and simply reflect on the stories - and what stories!

To give readers a flavour of the man, there follows a couple of tales that are typical of Nick's attitude to life, and subsequently of his approach to business. In these stories, as in the rest of the book, most of the names have been changed to protect the innocent and guilty alike - it has always been Nick's policy not to name people who are or have been involved in any way with the Clinic unless they have specifically given permission, or the events are a matter of public record.

Scandal

Nick left home at the age of 15 to seek fame and fortune in London's music scene. This was the early 1960s, when a singer-songwriter (like Nick) would sell a song for the price of a meal (or a drink), or see them plagiarised by powerful figures in the business. Even when topping the pop charts, a successful singer would earn a mere £20 a week. Luckily Nick came to the attention (in more ways than one) of Vanessa Heath, who was socially very well connected. Eventually taking him under her wing (and bedcovers), Vanessa launched her 'toy-boy' into the "better booking" scene, where he performed a 30-minute cabaret spot at prestigious events all over the country.

The organisation behind some of these 'gigs' was sloppy to say the least, which was surprising given the large amounts of money involved, the undoubted distinction of some of the venues, and at times the eminence of the hosts.

On one occasion Nick was handed a Park Drive cigarette packet, and written on the back in eyebrow pencil was the address of the venue. This turned out to be a stately pile set deep in the shires, later to become infamous as the setting of a major political scandal. His fee, ten times the national average weekly wage of the time, was stuffed inside the pack. The name of the nearest town was also scrawled on the packet, but due to lack of space the county wasn't mentioned. By coincidence (!) there was a town with a similar name just 20 miles from Nick's home. Only the sober but late attention of his father warned Nick that the actual venue was 150 miles south. He arrived at the big house with minutes to spare, and rushed to his dressing room with scarcely time to look around.

'Half cut,' because he was already abusing the booze, he staggered onto the stage in his white evening dress suit, face make-up slapped on quickly, guitar slung nonchalantly over his shoulder. Through the haze he vaguely remembered the wise words of an 'old-timer': "Always get a look at your audience before the curtain goes up. Never let what you are going to face come as a surprise." True to his mentor, Nick peeped casually through the curtains. They were all stark naked! Except, that is, for bow ties, socks and garters, and the odd tiara.

Nick turned to the compère in shock: "They're all bloody starkers." But the words froze on his lips - for the 'Master of Ceremonies' too stood before him as naked as a jaybird, apart from a red bow-tie mounted on white furred elastic. Before Nick could get any more words out, the outrageously gay MC chimed in. "Who's going to look a silly boy then, all dressed up like a dog's dinner in front of that lot!"

Being a pragmatist, and thinking of the money, Nick stripped off all his clothes, and performed his act with his guitar slung just slightly lower than usual. It was too late to do anything about his opening number ... "I want you to play with My Ding-a-Ling."

The Chaucer Marauders

There is far more to Nick's style of decision making than just pragmatic action. He is committed to putting his trust in the potential of the most unlikely bunch of people that have coalesced around him over the years, including utilising the talents (although not unconditionally) of the drunks from the Clinic. Just how he does it, and how far he will go, you will glean from the following small selection of his misadventures taken from the past four decades, both drunk and sober. Hopefully this will show those managers, who insist on complaining about the people below them in the corporate pecking order, that "they can find talent in the most unexpected of places." Nick insists "a failure to find and exploit that talent is most likely a failing of management, and not of the talent itself." So whenever managers feel justified in blaming their workforce, they should think again - think about the world of Nick Charles.

They should ponder how they would have dealt with the following situation from the early days of the Chaucer Clinic. The building that was to house the original clinic had no electricity, no running water, no heating, and the roof had 41 holes in it. After a minimum of preparation, the doors of Chaucer were to be opened for business one Monday. On the previous Friday a short article about Nick had appeared in the local newspaper, in which he invited anyone with a drink problem to help him set up a unit. Nick worked on the principle that the drunks couldn't be both working with him and drinking at the same time. The policy for all was strictly no booze, backed up with an expressed desire to work towards a sober life. "There's nothing wrong with them drinking like a fish, as long as they drink what the fish drinks."

Very soon the problems of refurbishing the desolate building he had taken on seemed insurmountable. He had no money - Nick was down to his last £12.50 since his show business career had finally given up on him. Undaunted, he welcomed the drunks as, in dribs and drabs, they started to arrive. Suddenly strange things began to happen. Electricity appeared miraculously at the flick of a switch; hot water gushed from rusty taps; the smell of bacon and eggs wafted from a brand new frying pan that was cooking on a mysteriously new stove; new tiles seemed to grow out of the walls; gallons of paint flowed like winter rain; there was more furniture than Pickfords could handle in a month of Sundays. It was a wonderful feeling to realise that there was so much help and generosity out there.

How did all this happen? You may well ask! Nick didn't realise it at the time, but the Chaucer Marauders had spontaneously combusted onto the scene. The first time it occurred to Nick that perhaps not all of the Clinic's benefactors were kosher was when two police officers arrived asking for a Mr Chasnick. It didn't need a Sherlock Holmes to make the connection with Nick Charles. The police were making enquiries concerning a suspicious receipt for several hundred pounds worth of building materials that had apparently been purchased by a Marauder who was now securely locked away in police custody. The offending document, which had obviously been printed with a child's 'John Bull' print set (remember this event took place long before the advent of desktop publishing), was the only proof of ownership to the van-load of materials. Nick, having no prior knowledge of any of the materials, gave a vague explanation of the Clinic's situation to the two officers. He apologised, adding that he had no control over the Marauder's exuberance.

The police explained that they were not concerned about the goods, or their destination. They were investigating the theft of a British Telecom van - the van that just happened to be trans-porting the materials to the Clinic. Under questioning, the Marauder in custody said he had just borrowed the van, and had every intention of returning it. Nick quickly organised a group of Marauders - those who weren't in jail - and off they went to unload the vehicle of its cargo. The van, complete with all its very expensive tools, was returned to BT. The accused pleaded insanity, and subsequently the Law in all its wisdom decided that the case was impossible to prosecute or defend. The Marauder eventually arrived safely back with Nick via a short stay at the local psychi-atric unit.

Thanks to the steady flow of building materials, the renovations continued apace. However, the roof was becoming the biggest problem, not because of a lack of supplies, but because they didn't have a ladder to get up there. Nick was not altogether surprised when a ladder suddenly materialised out of thin air, although he was somewhat sceptical when told that the Local Authority had donated it. Much later that same day the Director of Estates for the hospital (in whose grounds Chaucer was situated) arrived looking extremely angry. A very agitated and flustered Council worker accompanied him. Apparently the man had been stranded on a nearby roof for four hours before being rescued by a colleague. Someone had stolen his ladder while he was up there. The executive demanded to search the premises. Realising that possibly the game was up, and with eviction beckoning, Nick feigned complete surprise. Silently and reluctantly he accompa-nied the two on their search. Nothing! Finally, after having twice combed the building from end to end, they adjourned to the garden and searched behind shrubs and bushes. Still nothing!

Walking down the garden path towards the Clinic building Nick's blood froze as he caught sight of the black ladder overhanging a section of flat roof. The Estates Manager saw it too, and pointed it out to the workman. "Is that it George?"

"No," the man said immediately, "mine was a white-metalled aluminium lightweight." The Estates Manager mumbled a few half-hearted words of apology, and Nick courteously escorted the two men up the drive and off the property. On the way back to his office, Nick looked up at the ladder - wondering! He stood there in quiet contemplation when slowly, very slowly, a wet blob of black paint dripped mischievously onto his shoes!

The Chaucer Marauders had triumphed again! As for Nick Charles, he just quietly walked away.

Now if you want to learn more of Nick's triumphs, and his disasters, and just how he manages to 'treat those two impostors just the same,' then read on. For we are about to set out on the bumpy ride that is a guided tour of Nick's life.

Ian Angell

Introduction

Lamp-posts,
Lamp-posts everywhere

There is a drug that kills more Britons than heroin, cocaine, ecstasy, and all the other narcotics put together. It is responsible for hundreds of thousands of UK deaths each year - although most are officially put down to heart attacks, stokes, liver failure and the hundred and one other fatal symptoms of abusing the drug. Consequently, government figures put the annual death toll at a mere 30,000, a vast underestimate, so the full scale of the human catastrophe goes unnoticed. Under the drug's influence, hundreds of murders are carried out annually. It accounts for a third of wife-beaters and of baby-batterers. Through advertising, suppliers push that drug onto the young, despite knowing it may lead to a lifetime of addiction. The cost to the national economy in terms of lost hours of work, accidents, deaths and injury, damage to property, and health care is tens of billions of pounds annually. As for the people who peddle this drug, they make £2 billion each month in Britain alone, from which they make donations to political parties of all denominations, and for which they are immune from prosecution. That addictive drug is alcohol.

Nick Charles, an addict of alcohol, disintegrated into becoming a 'dosser' - street trash - and yet he eventually rejoined respectable society, rising like a phoenix from the ashes of social degradation, to become a successful entrepreneur. Before embarking on the exotic adventure that is Nick's life, I should first lay down the ground rules. Let me explain the common understanding that was the basis of our interviews about business issues, because that after all is what drove our conversations. Nick describes his world through stories; you might even call them parables - or maybe morality tales. I start with a story that encapsulates his view of 'Bureaucratic Management,' and is an ideal metaphor for making

his ideas clear for the reader. Nick identifies with all those poor
souls who have to suffer the excesses of the latest trendy management theories - indeed, that is why I dedicated this book to these
victims.

However, if that reader has no interest in the management issues
then I suggest they skip this Introduction, and move on directly to
Chapter 1, where the fun really begins.

Methodolics

It is two o'clock in the morning. A policeman sees a drunk scram-
bling around on his hands and knees under a street lamp. "Give
me your name," commands the officer. "Then who will I be?"
mumbles the drunk. Abandoning this fruitless tack, the policeman
demands to know what the drunk is doing. "I'm looking for my
keys, I lost them over there," he slurs, pointing into the darkness.
"So why look here?" asks the policeman. "Because this is where the
light is!" The sober policeman has been taught a valuable lesson,
one that every drunk already knows: lamp-posts are there for
support, NOT for illumination!

The behaviour of some of today's so-called managers has much in
common with the drunk's. The effect of the enormous stresses
placed on these managers (let's call them 'methodolics') will be
equated with what drives alcoholics into the pitiless clutches of
the demon drink. Promotion into the pressure cooker of management is intoxicating. Although it begins with a sense of high self-
esteem and euphoria, for many it can quickly degenerate into a
downward spiral towards a private hell of insecurity, panic and
hopelessness. This is why so many managers feel the urge to bask
in the wisdom shining down from the methodologies and
acronyms churned out by 'gurus' in the universities and business
schools: Management by Objectives (MBO), Business Process Re-
engineering (BPR), Knowledge Management (KM), Balanced
Score Card (BSC), Customer Relationship Management (CRM),
Enterprise Resource Management (ERM) to name just a few.
Lamp-posts all, primarily there for the support, and not for the
enlightenment of 'methodolics.'

Nonsense, you say! All these management approaches make
perfect sense! But then, to our drunk, his literal interpretations
and lateral thinking also make sense - of a sort! Perhaps drunks

know what the sober don't. Who can argue against the fact that the sole purpose of the light shining down from the lamp-post is to indicate its position, so that the unstable drunk can locate something to lean on. In this internally consistent alcoholic logic, the light is NOT there to illuminate the surrounding area. This metaphor is sadly all too appropriate for all those frantic methodolic managers who spend their working days staggering from the support of one trendy methodology to the next. Lamp-posts, lamp-posts everywhere, and any lamp-post will do. Ditto methodologies!

In their topsy-turvy world, drunks will value anything stable enough to lean against. But lamp-posts don't make their world any less topsy-turvy. And why is it topsy-turvy? Because they are drunk! What if the only difference between stressed methodolic managers and alcoholics is that eventually the drunks will realise that they are drunk, and that they must leave their false support to seek out help with the vicious circle of their addiction?

By the same token, stressed out and inebriated almost to the point of insensibility, methodolic managers become so confused that they don't know who they are, and dare not trust in their own sense of direction. Unable to cope with the responsibilities piling up on them, they "don't know which way is up," and so they lean against the nearest source of stability. They stagger along from one business gimmick (from one theoretical lamp-post) to another, in the vain hope that the next will enlighten their actions. Methodolics don't ask: "how come there are so many answers being proposed for business problems? How come so many lamp-posts?" For "when a lot of different remedies are proposed for a disease, that means the disease can't be cured" (Chekov, The Cherry Orchard, 1904). Perhaps the plethora of business remedies highlights the disease, rather than cures it! Rather than guide, maybe these lamps misguide?

We should ask whether the prevailing light of management wisdom is capable of illuminating the pressures and uncertainties that all businesses face. Indeed, scrabbling around in the glare emanating from management gurus can even make the pressure worse, particularly when the methodolic manager looks to the light, rather than to where the keys of appropriate action are to be found - out there in the darkness.

How bizarre to believe that the stress in the business world can be made controllable by enlightened methodical acts of management? The certainties of life shine on yesterday, but not on tomorrow. No lamp-post can illuminate success in the future. Control is a myth; just another example of the victory of hope over experience, and even that experience tends only to appear long after it was needed. There is no control, only control freaks! The business gurus who tell us that they have all the answers are deluded. The natural human condition is having to cope with the world as it is and is becoming (including toiling with the excesses of control freaks), rather than being in control of it. Perhaps astute managers should crawl around in the darkness to find the keys to their problems, and should trust to their own insights as they search for success. The best advice is to wise up, sober up, and move away from the phoney illumination of methodological certainties.

Nick's Approach to Business

The following chapters will follow through on this thesis, namely that the drunk's actions have much in common with the stressed modern manager. This metaphor will be expanded to consider how these managers tend to perceive the difficulties they all must face when keeping their particular shows on the road.

Consequently, the book deliberately sets out to take a sideways look at the monolith of modern management, but from a drunk's perspective. Of course, the particular drunk in question is Nick Charles. Although Nick has been 'on the wagon' for nearly thirty years, he can still think like a drunk, and that skill has sharpened his sense of the ridiculous. And ridiculous is the only word to describe so much of today's management theory. However, given my enthusiasm for telling Nick's anecdotes, it was inevitable that this management theme should end up as a subtext - an important subtext, but a subtext none the less. First and foremost this is a biography.

Nick's personal approach to running his business is to accept with equanimity whatever the world has to throw at him, and then to take advantage of whatever comes to hand with the help of a vast network of contacts, all the while trying to minimise the hazards. But "no more lamp-posts." He recognises that "necessity is the mother of innovation as well as invention." So how does Nick take advantage of what is necessarily so? By looking at each new predicament in novel ways, and seizing the moment. He always starts by recognising that the business world is an illogical place that only stressed methodolic managers and drunks think is rational. In accepting his already confused state, Nick is not disturbed by the confusing nature of the world. He just accepts it and gets on with life, one moment at a time, always realising that he is operating on the edge and that his business can go "belly-up" at any time.

By watching the predictable behaviour of the deluded and drunken alcoholic/methodolic automatons around him, Nick believes it is possible to re-interpret their actions to advantage. He is quite clear that all of humanity, the sober as well as the drunk, spend their lives leaning on metaphorical lamp-posts - only the drunks come to realise the fact. And they know that everything in human experience is ambiguous. Trying to make unambiguous what is intrinsically ambiguous is a crazy and futile quest.

We must all admit that our theories are looking in the wrong place for enlightenment, for there is no such location as 'the right place.' Just like the poor and deluded drunken fools lost in the bottle, we don't even know that we're lost.

The sober too must find their way in this uncertain world. Should the sober be lucky enough to find something useful in the penumbra from the light of a theory, then that's a bonus. Utility comes despite the light, not because of it. "What convinces us is not necessarily true, it is merely convincing" (Nietzsche).

Therefore, this book does NOT lay a business theory out before readers, for that would be to reject Nick's fundamental position. He is certain that the complexity of human experience cannot be categorised with simplistic tables, naïve checklists of advice, or catalogues of rules. Businesses prosper by building on the experience of having survived the complexity of past successes and failures. That experience comes from an awareness of being in the world, not from hiding behind some artificially constructed methodological expertise. Such expertise, although necessary in (but not sufficient for) certain contrived situations (such as accounting, managing computers or conforming to regulations), has to be transcended when dealing with day-to-day events.

Consequently this book sets out to tell anecdotes, morality tales, from the complexity of Nick's life. He then expects the reader to share that experience. For in these anecdotes, Nick neatly encapsulates his approach to the problems he has faced, and solved (so far), both in business and in life - problems that will resonate among most managers as echoes of their own particular situations. Therefore, in many cases it is left to those managers themselves to synthesize their own lessons from the stories, and for each of them to take whatever business morals are relevant to their own particular and unique conditions - morals, therefore, that would not even occur to Nick or myself.

Just because Nick may initiate a stream of ideas, that doesn't mean he will share their interpretation. For it is the curse of humanity, and its blessing, that the world is necessarily one of incomplete and asymmetric information. Nick tells the story of the farmer who owned a pumpkin patch, and was furious that a certain delinquent from the neighbourhood would steal his produce. The farmer hatched a cunning plan. He put up a notice saying: "One of these pumpkins has been injected with cyanide." That should stop the thefts he thought. A little later he heard a commotion in his patch, and so he charged out. All the pumpkins were still there, but the sign had been defaced. The word 'One' had been crossed out and replaced by 'Two.'

We will, we must, make assumptions when interpreting this partial information, and hence we jump to personal conclusions when dealing with it. Others respond using their own interpretations. The human condition is unequivocally one of bizarre social constructions that are experienced differently by each of us.

Therefore, to run a business, we must each make our own way in the world, differently, by gleaning as much information as we can from the dimly lit conditions around us, and we must live with the consequences. However, there can be no clear objectivity in data when people are involved. For objectivity falls apart the moment we enter the realm of a perverse humanity. Consequently, the approach of this book is necessarily highly subjective, and it contains no apologies for that. Therefore, an appropriate reading of this book depends heavily on each reader interpreting the rhetoric of the storyteller via his/her own unique personal experiences. The business world, like all human activity, is full of noise.

Noise is spontaneous, and in the noisy battleground where rhetoric confronts logic, rhetoric always wins. Therefore, we must never approach any situation with a preconceived notion of what is logical or illogical, rational or irrational. Treat every moment on its merits. Live with uncertainty, and love it.

1

A Booze-up in a Brewery

We've all been there, suffering the consequences of the actions of some fool or other who couldn't organise a booze-up in a brewery. From all sectors of society, in every (disorganised!) organisation, in every business, there are those arrogant and ignorant people (usually stressed-out methodolic men - that's right MEN) who seem to create confusion in everything they touch. Somehow unwittingly they manage to make things worse, even when they are operating in perfectly non-problematic and benign situations.

Things can only get much worse when these people are dropped into a hazardous environment, for then they are a real menace. Unfortunately, many of them occupy very senior positions in commercial enterprises, as the world's shareholders and pensioners have learned to their cost over recent years. The overpaid methodolics in charge of business have no idea what to do now that their methods no longer cope with the risk implicit in a changing and uncertain world. This does beg the question that if all they were doing was blindly following ritualised methods, why were they paid such huge salaries?

Thankfully there are some individuals who know how to deal with RISK, and who seem to thrive on it. Nick is such a person - someone about whom it can truly be said that he knows all there is to know about booze-ups and breweries. We will look at how Nick came to found his clinic, and at his subsequent experiences. Hopefully the analysis will provide useful lessons about the underlying principles by which he manages Chaucer Clinic; a balancing act, as he would be the first to admit, 'on the edge of chaos.' Running a clinic for alcoholics! Now that really is a risky business. Day in, day out, he tries to help violent anti-social substance abusers, who often don't want helping, from a society that has little patience with, and even less understanding of drunks. That is no picnic.

But that's not all! How does he pay for it all? The political parties of all colours, while mouthing supportive sentiments, have successively withdrawn financial support from those who try to help alcoholics. So how does Nick cope with the uncertainty, when even the day-to-day existence of his clinic is an ever-present headache? How does he get up in the morning and drag himself into another (possibly violent) day at the office, not even knowing if the office will even be there next week? Will Chaucer still be open when this book is published? What keeps him going? What stops him running away, screaming? The answers to these and other similar questions, and the lessons to be learnt from someone who can deal effectively under this type of pressure are of value to stressed managers everywhere who want to stay off the 'methodol.'

The Start of a Friendship

So let's start with our hero Nick Charles. He and I are neighbours. One day in 1995 I was standing in my garage entrance casually looking across at the removal van parked outside the house opposite, pretending not to be curious about the new neighbours (as you do!). Suddenly a gleaming red Jaguar drove up, and out they popped. Nick came over directly, and started talking - it seems to me that he hasn't stopped since. He introduced himself as Nick Charles and his wife Kelly Miller. Odd I thought: "how American, using hyphenated forenames Nick-Charles; or perhaps Mr Charles wasn't married to Mrs Miller?" - but that's another story (see below). The situation got even more complicated as I was soon to find out that there were two other important women in Nick's life, Teresa and Nikki - and yet more stories, but that's for later chapters.

Conversation quickly gravitated to Nick's new car (as you do!), and admiration for the beautiful machine flowed unbounded from us both. Absentmindedly, I took out my handkerchief and began polishing the left rear-side window. In the bright sunshine I had spotted two parallel lines of dark dots on the glass. The dots wouldn't come off despite all my elbow grease. Nick tried too, and failed. This was hardly surprising, since the marks weren't shadows on the window at all. The two of us were looking through the window at a discolouration of the leather upholstery. Mary (my wife), who had joined us by now, brought some furniture polish - Nick and Kelly hadn't yet unpacked. The marks still didn't budge. To cut a long story short, the shadows turned out to be scars caused by stitch marks, the memory of a long-gone operation on the hide of the cow that had donated the leather. The Jaguar Motor Company immediately replaced the whole back seat, and sales executive, Paul Evans tells the tale to this day, thereby ensuring that the story of a ghostly apparition on a cow's carcass has entered the folklore of Jaguar franchisees. This could only happen to a customer like Nick Charles!

It didn't take long for Nick to introduce himself as "the drunk who runs the Chaucer Clinic in Ealing," fully expecting that I had heard of it. Seeing that I knew next to nothing of alcoholism and the alcoholic, he immediately started recounting some very colourful stories of his days as a 'dosser.' Noticing the dubious expression on my face and unabashed, Nick offered to lend me 'The Diaries of Brummie Nick.' He had written down the stories on scraps of paper and old exercise books as he was taking his first faltering steps towards sobriety. These were the basis of the cathartic healing process in which he pulled himself up from the depths of degradation to rejoin normality. Nick had recently had his memoirs typed up and loosely bound in a folder; with this treasure (?) under my arm I walked away from our first encounter.

Such was the start of our unlikely friendship, and my almost insignificant introduction into what I now recognise as the surreal world of Nick Charles (or is it Miller?) Now whenever we meet, I wait expectantly for a colourful description of the latest complexity surrounding Nick. This surprises Nick because he doesn't see anything strange in the rollercoaster that is his life. He is used to odd things happening around him. As a magnet to peculiar phenomena, he takes it all in his stride. "Don't similar situations happen to everyone?" Well they do to everyone who knows Nick! For they too tend to be sucked in to his crazy world.

Like the time in 1998 when my wife and I, along with Nick's long-time agent Kenneth Earle, went to the Hilton Hotel in London as Nick and Kelly's guests at a Gala Award Ceremony for Entrepreneurs in the Care Industry. Nick was one of four nominees chosen from a list of hundreds. The evening started with us all getting lost, and eventually parking on the wrong side of a busy road to the hotel. While waiting to cross to the Hilton we were caught in a sudden torrential downpour. Bedraggled, our group finally sat down to dinner ... just as the hotel caught fire. Alarms bells were ringing everywhere. The main electric power supply failed. Thankfully the dining room was away from the source of the fire - but the kitchen wasn't. We sat there in the semi-darkness of emergency lighting, eating a cold starter and some cake - the main course remained partially cooked in the kitchen.

The show, however, did go on, rescued only by the skilled profes-sionalism of radio celebrity Nicholas Parsons. Fire-warden's megaphone in hand, on a barely lit stage, he ad-libbed his way through the prize-giving with an amazing spontaneous perform-ance, bouncing jokes off a bemused stooge he had plucked from among the hotel employees. Here was proof, if proof were needed, of Nick's insistence that "the ability to deal with uncer-tainty and surprise cannot be taught, it is an intrinsic skill fine-tuned by experience - experience and not expertise."

Management of Uncertainty

Complexity surrounds Nick. It searches him out. Over the years I have become fascinated by how Nick is un-phased by disaster, and manages to survive and prosper against this background - and Nick has prospered, witness the Jag.' The more we got to know each other, the more I asked myself: "What is his secret?" "How does Nick manage in what are conditions of almost total uncertainty" I became increasingly intrigued as a perplexed Nick calmly told me: "we all live in exactly the same world, only I'm more aware of the extremes. And they are more aware of me!"

"And they are more aware of me!" That seemingly odd statement rang bells with me, and I immediately concluded that there was something useful to be learned from Nick's way of doing things. As a professor of Information Systems at the London School of Economics, I am expected to lecture on a broad range of business topics including the management of uncertainty and of risk.

Over the years I have become extremely irritated by the so-called scientific approaches to uncertainty that are being peddled by the self-styled gurus of the academic community. I have observed that, when faced with profound uncertainty, the knee-jerk reaction in most companies is to try and manage that uncertainty by using some half-baked management theory, rather than accepting uncertainty as a necessary fact of life, and then just dealing with it in a pragmatic way. The managements of these companies don't seem to have learned the lesson that they may only use a theory effectively when they are already well predisposed towards it. The arbitrary use of an ill-suited theory is likely to cause more trouble than it's worth.

My view has always been that the uncertainty faced by business does not conform to any neat logic. It is a foreboding, where the surprise of imminent change is outside management control. It bears repeating: control is a myth! I was once at a commercial conference entitled 'Managing Uncertainty,' where the technology session consisted of myself, and a statistician. The statistician talked for forty-five minutes on distributions, expectations, functions, formulae and curves; inspiring stuff for a business audience! Within five minutes eyes began to glaze over. After ten minutes he was just talking to an audience of one: me. I was on the stage, and so I had to listen to the nonsense.

When it was my turn, I walked over to the podium, and just stood there, ... and stood there, ... and stood there. For a whole minute I just stood there. I fidgeted uneasily, and shot frantic and terrified glances at the audience. At first there was silence, then a few murmurs, then a growing rumble of concern. The chairman rose to help. He was half-way across the stage when I banged my fist on the table, and said: "Now that is uncertainty, it has nothing to do with statistics." Business is like poker; there's a lot of bluffing going on. Players who put all their faith in the statistical distribution of the cards will surely lose. "People who view humanity through the lens of statistics believe that the average human being has one tit and one testicle."

Uncertainty is nothing to do with randomness or chaos - quite the opposite. For chaos disappears into the background as white noise - we pass right through it unnoticed. Uncertainty, on the other hand, is all about order, but it is an unwelcome order, a strangeness, that arises from an unexpected and surprising conspiracy of events. The world inhabited by humanity is intrinsically strange, fantastical, and we are deluding ourselves if we think that we can always make sense of that strangeness. We merely collect all the strange events together under this label of uncertainty, and hope that they will go away. 'Managing Uncertainty' is just another futile attempt at coping with the conspiracy of strangeness. The order in uncertainty is unwelcome because it approaches us out of the darkness. It doesn't sit nicely in the authoritarian glare of some theoretical lamp-post.

There is no ignoring this strangeness in the human condition, as it inevitably returns to bite us. Uncertainty holds the seeds of both opportunity and hazard. Suddenly the (very trendy) word 'Risk' raises its ugly head. 'Taking a Risk' is at the core of all business, namely the search to profit from opportunities, all the while minimizing hazards. Stressed methodolic managers, however, only see themselves and their companies as being 'at Risk.'

When it comes to teaching my students about uncertainty, and of risk, I avoid the many dubious methodological theories. Of course I have to teach them about methods, but I warn them - "you must learn about methods just like medical students learn about venereal disease." I believe risk must be handled at a personal level. Consequently, I prefer the pragmatism of anecdotes, leaving it to my students to formulate their own insights. Increasingly, as I was searching for an antidote that would inoculate my students against the false certainties of management theories, I began to mention Nick in my lectures. Here was an example of someone managing on the sharp edge of real uncertainty. For when he was drunk Nick had to survive in a very strange world indeed; the drunk sees nothing unusual with the world being strange - it is the natural state.

I began to wonder whether Nick, as a sober drunk with his weird memories, is perhaps better predisposed to deal with all the uncertainty in the world; an uncertainty that refuses to be ignored. The students found this a welcome change from the normal fodder of management literature: contrived statistical examples, the nonsense of competitive advantage that is supposedly gained by applying computerised information systems, and from reminiscences of 'great men.' In Nick, I thought, here was a man who deals successfully with real uncertainty, truly weird situations, on a daily basis. Just how weird, and how effective his operating style is, will become clear as this book progresses.

Nick and Kelly

"What was Nick's management style?" I asked. "Did he have a clear idea of what he was doing, or was he a 'natural,' blessed with a sixth sense, a frame of mind for dealing with adversity and perversity?" I finally came to the conclusion that the answer was 'a bit of both.' Never having come across such a colourful character before, I have subsequently realised that there aren't many people like Nick around. The rest of us have a lot to learn from such an individual. That was why I eventually asked Nick whether he objected to his management style being used as a case study in my lectures, and subsequently how I ended up writing this book.

Before we start, let's get one thing out of the way immediately. Nick Charles has been married to Kelly Miller for thirty years. Nick Charles's real name is Nicholas Charles Miller, and there is nothing sinister about his alias. When Nick chose to become a pop singer in the late nineteen-fifties there were five significant Millers travelling the circuit, including another Nick. He needed a different stage name - and that name has stuck. Simple! Well, nothing about Nick is simple.

His wife Kelly was Kelly Miller long before she met Nick, even though her given name is Lesley Roach. After a career as a child actress, appearing in such films as *Oliver, Moon over the Alley, The Year of the Sex Olympics*, and dozens of West End theatre productions and TV commercials. Lesley went on to become a television actress and then a singer. She took her stage name mixing the name Kelly from the TV programme *Charlie's Angels*, and Miller from the carpet company (?). Just who was promising to take whom as their lawfully wedding spouse made their wedding ceremony surreal. Nick manages to get tangled in such coincidences, oddities, misunderstandings, and complexities without even trying.

But we are running ahead of ourselves. The most important thing to know about Nick is that he was a drunk. He would say he IS a drunk. "Once a drunk, always a drunk; the trick is to stay sober!" However, half an hour before noon on Monday the 13th of December 1976, just two days short of his thirty-second birthday, he chose sobriety; and hasn't looked back since. On the other hand, I am teetotal, and always have been. Nick at first thought that I was another dried-out alcoholic, since "there are three types of teetotaller: ex-alcoholics, religious spoilsports, and those with problems with alcoholics in the family." However, I am an atheist, with no family history of alcoholism, and with no view one way or the other on alcohol. I have never ever taken an alcoholic drink, and have no conception of the urge to drink. Nick was only half-joking when he said: "And you think that I'm weird!" Needless to say, he was as much intrigued by my peculiar behaviour, as I was by his.

Back to our story! Drunk or sober, Nick could talk the birds down from the trees. Thankfully he now uses that charm to good effect. When he was a drunk, like all addicts, he used it cynically to manipulate family and friends in support of his habit. Perversely, many of the skills for manipulating and influencing those around him, which he honed to perfection as a drunk, he has used constructively to run the Chaucer Clinic. Who knows?

Perhaps an alcoholic has a shrewd insight into the workings of human nature? After all, drunks have to survive in the most unlikely of circumstances. They have to innovate continually in order to deal with their own drunken and peculiar interpretation of a sober real world. Furthermore, the newly sober, having survived years of degradation, have seen it all, and have no delusions about the human condition.

From this starting point I set out to unravel the wisdom of Nick Charles, discovering a mixture of pragmatism and scepticism, a synthesis of his experiences, drunk and sober. It was clear from the beginning that Nick does not operate on the basis of some preconceived rulebook of dos and don'ts. He is an alcoholic, but he is no methodolic! Nick's approach is NOT some self-conscious intellectual process, rather it is direct action grounded in his personal sense of appropriateness. However, ask Nick to define 'appropriate' and he will respond "I can't define an elephant, but I know one when I see one."

To Nick, life is packed full of ambiguity. He doesn't believe it possible to avoid the inevitable ensuing uncertainty by hiding behind some all-embracing method. Rather, he embraces uncertainty, treating each unique situation on its own merits, trusting in his own insights to deal with it. What this means is that he develops a sense of appropriateness based firmly on personal experience, and not expertise gleaned from books, and on the willingness to trust in one's natural and immediate response to each novel situation.

What follows is a story of uncertainty, but not the nice tidy stuff that forms the typical core of much of today's business advice. Our tale, albeit extreme, is an acceptance of the nasty and messy everyday conditions that are faced in life and business. This will be an expression of the personal choices, decisions and actions that were responsible for a journey to hell, and back. On that journey Nick has learned a very important lesson: the only lamp-posts he can really rely on for support are himself, and a small band of friends and colleagues who have earned his trust.

2

Nick's Fall from Grace

I must make one thing crystal clear from the start. Neither Nick nor I set out here to recommend alcoholism as a management-training scheme, some kind of alternative MBA (Master of Business Administration) programme! There can be NO Management By Alcohol. We both realise that the business world is already full of bad managers, made worse by drink: the Chaucer Clinic has housed more than its fair share. (By the same token Nick believes the world is full of bad managers, some made worse by method.) There is no way that Nick (and I, both committed teetotallers) would promote an excess of alcohol (or method) as a virtue.

This book sets out to describe the thinking of just one drunk, and that particular drunk certainly wouldn't recommend his learning curve to anyone. For our hero once woke up in a sewer, having been stabbed in the stomach, with rats eating his congealed blood! On another occasion, barely conscious but catatonic with drink, he was dumped into a body-bag and nearly carted off to the morgue for a post mortem. Terrifying! And not for the faint hearted. However, such experiences do tend to put all other situations into perspective. It is easy to see how Nick can be pragmatic about minor problems such as cash flow crises in the order of the odd hundred thousand pounds.

Nick's story takes him through highs and lows: from the high of being honoured by the Queen at Buckingham Palace, down to when he awoke to find himself the main course for vampire rats. But let's start at the beginning of this journey to the bottom ... and back. On the downward journey, Nick was witness to suicides, accidental deaths and murders; he even bought his life for a pound, an incident clearly recounted in his book, *Through A Glass Brightly*. Consequently he has no illusions about the value of human life. Nick has suffered fractures of his skull and numerous other bones, and even frostbite (in England!) His body still bears the scars of numerous stabbings and other wounds: deliberate, accidental and self-inflicted. It was a long way down to the sheer helplessness and hopelessness of the gutters in Skid Row, a fall punctuated by numerous false dawns.

The Wrong Side of The Tracks

That part of Nick's story is stuffed full with pathos and farce. Like the time he tried to commit suicide. Picture the scene, one Sunday in March, of Nick, worse for drink, spread-eagled semi-conscious across a railway track. Hour, after hour he waited patiently for the train that would come along to end it all. Nick waited, and waited, and waited. Eventually the drink wore off, and he really began to suffer from cramp caused by lying in this very uncomfortable position. He picked himself up, dusted himself off, and staggered down the line to the nearby railway station. There he found an official notice informing the public that, as from that particular weekend, the railway-company had decided to cancel all Sunday passenger services until further notice. Pragmatically he did what all drunks do: he broke into a nearby shed and found a place to sleep. Moments later he awoke with a start as a goods train came rumbling along the line! It's not surprising, therefore, that Nick has a belief in his own indestructibility. Perhaps somebody up there really does love him.

Without question, Nick's story is extreme. Yet he insists that it is still an everyday story; one that every manager could recognise as his own. The very fact that the story is so extreme means the essence of each ridiculous situation is so much easier to identify. Wrapped up in the customary noise of business, most managers find it more difficult to put their fingers on the specific concerns that haunt them. Hence their search for certainty, and their consequent addiction with business methods that promise security. Like all addicts, methodolics want their fix, and they don't care where they get it. The downward spiral begins. The first step out of the mire is recognising their addiction, and wanting to get out of it. They must choose to enter a detox(ification) process, followed by a rehabilitation programme, before starting to live life to the full.

Both Nick and I want readers to think of this book as a 'detox and rehab' in itself. By mapping Nick's anecdotes onto their own personal experience, we want managers to recognise what is ridiculous in their personal circumstances, and to understand their perverse situation as a necessary and inevitable condition of business. It will not be easy. A British Prime Minister, Sir Harold Macmillan, was once asked what was the most difficult part of politics. His reply: "Events, dear boy, events." It's the same in business; it's the same in life. There can be no easy rational solution to the ludicrous events that are out there, all conspiring in the darkness of uncertainty. To deal with all the nonsense the methodolic manager must sober up, so that he can accept what is necessarily so, and then go on to invent pragmatic and practical decisions that can deal with all the absurdity.

However, before we can start the detox by considering Nick's approach to managing Chaucer Clinic, it is essential that we first fill in the background, as his experiences prior to sobriety go some way to explaining the attitudes that colour his actions. In the next few chapters we will cover much of his first thirty-two years at a pace, before getting down to the nitty gritty. So let's start at the beginning. Nick was born on December 15th 1944 in Langley, near Birmingham, and spent all his formative years in the Midlands. His father was a policeman, and his mother was … his mother. In those days women were homemakers. Nick's mother doted on her prodigal son. Consequently he had a very happy childhood; so he has no excuses for his fall from grace. He still feels a great shame for the disappointment he caused his mother, and guilt for the fact that she died before she could witness his redemption.

The Amplifier and the Football Club

Nick was blessed with a good singing voice, and soon gravitated to the popular music culture that was beginning to thrive in England in the late nineteen-fifties. Ever conscious of his father's job, Nick would go to extremes to be accepted as 'one of the lads.' He quickly developed a skill for humour, and through it, social manipulation. The first signs of Nick's silver tongue came in early 1958. A thirteen year-old, he was playing in a local band that couldn't afford an amplifier. They had to bang all hell out of their acoustic guitars just to be heard. At the end of one particularly well-received performance Nick pounced: "How about having a whip-round for an amplifier?" Over the following weeks they collected fifty pounds. Nick's father generously put up the rest. From that point on, he was hooked. Education would take a back seat. Nick had made up his mind: he would be a 'pop singer.'

The Birth of an Entrepreneur

Nick the entrepreneur appeared a year later. He was (and still is) a fanatical supporter of Aston Villa Football Club - oh well, I didn't say he was perfect. The team had a midweek match that he was unable to attend. Late in the evening a very impatient Nick rang the club, and eagerly asked for the result. "Look in the morning papers," was the curt response. He was furious, and decided there and then to complain about his treatment to Eric Houghton, the team manager.

In the 12-page foolscap letter he didn't stop at complaining. He listed a whole raft of suggestions for how the club, idolised by many thousands, could improve their image and at the same time initiate money-making schemes to bring the club additional income: replica shirts, signed photographs, a restaurant at the ground, an Aston Villa newspaper containing players' biographies etc. The letter was handed over personally to the 'Villa management' by a family friend with connections at the club: Mr Onslow, a Kidderminster greengrocer. Even at the tender age of fourteen Nick understood the importance of networks. The reply came back two weeks later. It praised Nick's imagination, but gently informed him that such crazy ideas could never happen in the game of football! In hindsight, he also learned that good timing is everything. Having a vision thirty years ahead of its time is as worthless as being blind to opportunity.

The Golden Wonder

By now Nick was treading water in school. He just wanted to leave as soon as possible, confident that he could successfully travel the road to fame and fortune in the pop music business. Little did he imagine that it would turn out to be the road to ruin. He left school soon after his fifteenth birthday, in December 1959, willing to take on whatever job would come along, just to fill in time and to pay his way. He had already started out as a semi-professional singer, and this is where he focused his energies. Nick even travelled to London in search of success together with 'Pete,' one of his fellow band-members from the Zodiacs.

However, 'Pete' soon abandoned Nick to join a group called the Tornados, who went on to have a huge worldwide hit with *Telstar*. Nick returned to the Midlands with his tail between his legs, but with his thirst for fame unquenched, although his naïve trust in fair-weather friends was badly dented.

It was two years later, at the age of seventeen, when his father took him for his first 'real drink' down at the Black Boy Public House in Bewdley, Worcestershire. Nick says he was an alcoholic from day one; all alcoholics are alcoholics from day one. He tells the apocryphal tale of villages in France a hundred years ago where eight-year-old children were lined up and each given a glass of wine. From their immediate reactions the villagers apparently knew instinctively which children were going to be the drunkards. Then they kept a close eye on those who were likely to be problematic in the years to come.

Nick was still not making enough money from his singing to turn fully professional at this point, and so he decided to take a job as a sales-representative with the Golden Wonder Crisp Company. Nick can sell refrigerators to Eskimos. It wasn't long before he was 'salesman of the year,' coming to the attention of the management. They were planning to make (what today we would call) a corporate video. Nick had self-promoted his experience in the 'entertainment business' within the company, and so it was only natural that he was asked to play a major role in the film, part of which was also turned into a television advertisement. He was on his way up; that is until his need for alcohol surpassed both his need for employment, and even the call of fame. It didn't take long for him to be categorised and fired as an unreliable drunk, who had managed to wreck a number of company vans. In total, over a fourteen-month period, at Golden Wonder and with other companies, he managed to write-off fourteen automobiles - one a month!

Come Fly with Me

Meanwhile Nick was gradually succeeding in his show-business career, and this brought him into contact with some of its celebrities. He spent one particularly boozy afternoon with a member of an internationally famous rock group, who had just bought a Piper light aircraft and was embarking on a series of lessons at a local airfield. The star, so full of his plane, and like Nick well-oiled, decided to show off his proud possession.

They pushed it out of the hangar for a closer inspection, and Nick's new pal started the engine. Soon they were sitting together, chugging gently around the airfield, which was bounded on three sides by quiet country lanes, with a main road completing a rectangle. Nick begged to try, and soon he was heading towards a hedge that separated the field from the dual carriageway, quite some distance ahead. He didn't see the field suddenly fall away down a steep bank. The engine stalled on Nick, but the momentum still sent the aircraft careering into the hedge.

The plane suffered only minor damage, however, it would be quite a shove to get it back up the bank. Nick had a brainwave. They would push it through a nearby five-bar gate, onto the dual carriageway, down the road fifty yards, and then through another gate back onto the field where the bank had flattened out. The plane went through the gate easily enough, and onto the road. Of course, the reason why there was no bank fifty yards along was that the road had an uphill gradient.

Not for the last time would Nick come to realise that so-called solutions can be a restatement of the original problem, but in a different form. That new form can end up making things worse. The effort of pushing the aircraft was too much for the two of them, and after several noble attempts they sank exhausted onto the kerb. Thankfully the road traffic was light, and there was just enough room for astonished drivers to squeeze their cars under the plane's wing.

Then Nick had another brainwave: "We'll drive it! That's the answer, we'll drive it!" The rock star was now fast asleep and in no condition to care. With Nick at the helm, the plane went quietly chugging up the road. Then he heard the sound of a siren, and thought: "I must get a move on to let the ambulance through."

The police officer, who had left the patrol car, blue lights still flashing, walked slowly up to the plane. "I'm not going to believe this am I?" The tone wasn't unfriendly, so Nick cheerfully asked if he would push them back onto the airfield. The officer looked first at the two dishevelled aeronauts, then at the traffic, and called his partner over. Thanks to the boys-in-blue the aircraft was soon safely back where it belonged, on the airfield. "Have you been drinking?"

By now the inebriated rock star had woken up: "Officer, it's my plane, and we were in a real fix. No harm's been done. Please give us a break."

The officer paused momentarily: "I'm not sure if there's anything in the book to cover drunk in charge of an aeroplane on a main arterial road, however, ..." He reached for his pocket book, and with a sly grin whispered to the plane's owner: "Can I have your autograph?"

Wash 'n' Dry

Despite the booze, his singing career was progressing well. The young Nick Charles was lucky enough to sign a contract with a major recording company. The management of the record label, very forward thinking for the pop business, was concerned about the longevity of the careers of young singers on their books. Their policy was that all recording artists under the age of seventeen should take on a second trade. There were four trades on offer: car mechanic, office administration, electrician, and ladies hairdressing. Nick, being Nick, chose the fourth option. Having undertaken some arduous research in his locality, he had quickly realised that hairdressing salons employed the best female 'talent' around.

His management had decided that he would attend a salon in Mayfair to learn the skills of colouring, cutting and styling. On his first day he was up at the crack of dawn, anticipating exciting times with his beautiful new workmates. Imagine his reaction when he was introduced to his tutor, a young, handsome, but extremely gay Neville.

The entertainment business is nothing if not precarious. During one particularly long spell 'resting,' Nick used his newly found skills to land the job as a representative for Schwarzkopf, selling their world-renowned hair-products to salons across the Midlands. The company was very generous with demonstration stock supplied to their 'reps.' There were upwards of 500 salons on his relatively small territory, and it didn't take Nick long to discover that a high proportion was barely making a living. Their rents were high, hair care products phenomenally expensive, and competition fierce. Salons seemed to come and go at an alarming rate, and so Nick hatched a plan. He approached a likely target and suggested a partnership. They would retain 51% of the equity of the business, he would take 49% and supply all materials: after all he had plenty to spare. Nick was a great salesman: it wasn't long before he had 26 salons in his empire. Meanwhile nobody in the German company looked too closely at his stock keeping, because he was a star salesman.

It was the booze that finally got him fired, and eventually brought down his burgeoning salon empire. Nick found it impossible to get out of bed before lunchtime! However, the real cruncher was the fact that he had written off four of their company cars.

Down and Out

No longer in receipt of free samples, Nick kept his empire afloat for a short time by manufacturing his own shampoo, and supplying it by the gallon to salons. He mixed the shampoo upstairs in his mother's bathtub, adding his own perfume. Nick had connected the waste pipe to a rubber hose in the downstairs kitchen. He would pull out the bath plug and rush downstairs to fill gallon containers while sitting on a kitchen stool. This enterprise came to an end when his father, tired of the inconvenience, insisted on bathing on a regular basis!

Then he went on to work for Simoniz, and next Bex Bissell. Very successful at the start in each of his new companies, Nick's boozing made sure that no employment lasted very long. The singing didn't help either, because whenever he was offered a 'gig,' he would drop everything at his job and charge off, knowing that this time he would be famous.

One low high-point of his salesmanship was with his next employers, Frenlite Flour Mills, of Ware in Hertfordshire. He was working the Birmingham area for them, when he managed to sell four 'outers' of flour to a Chinese Restaurant in Wolverhampton. Each 'outer' contained a quarter tonne of flour! The proprietors were expecting four two-pound bags of flour as samples. Having no idea that a tonne of flour was on its way, they were devastated when a huge lorry turned up with their purchase.

But then there were the low low-points. The area manager of the firm was, like Nick, an alcoholic. Nick happened to be with him when he tried to withdraw money from his personal bank account at Barclays Bank in a suburb of Birmingham, only to be told that he was overdrawn and no money was forthcoming. Not an unusual event in the life of a drunk! Furious, the area manager screamed and shouted, and was physically ejected from the bank. So he started taking it out on Nick. The people of Kings Norton still talk about the two drunks who had a flour fight in the High Street, covering everything for a quarter mile in a fine white dust. Neither man lasted much longer with the company.

There were other jobs, but the time span between hiring and firing was getting shorter and shorter, until eventually employment wasn't even an option. Nick was down and out on Skid Row.

3

Hitting Rock Bottom

Sitting down, listening to Nick tell his stories, I still can't escape comparing the now with the then, contrasting today's Nick with the Old Nick on the streets. Today's Nick is still just as much a magnet for chaos and complexity, but his values are so very different. Now he stresses the importance of personal trust-relationships and decency. Back then Nick systematically cheated everyone in his rapidly diminishing circle of acquaintances.

Every addict learns the golden rule of the confidence trickster very early in their addiction: "Steal from family and friends first." If you can steal from those nearest and dearest to you, then you will cheat everybody else without a second thought. To give an idea of just how low Nick could go, a very loud American tourist once caught him trying to steal money from an open donation plate in St Paul's Cathedral!

During those times Nick would manage to stay sober long enough to raise sufficient funds to rent a place to stay, usually for a few months, before the next 'bender' would find him evicted. He would then beg friends to put him up for a few weeks. As he became more and more of a nuisance, and they tired of him, the period between evictions was reduced to a few days; friends became fewer and fewer. Eventually they would telephone ahead to warn each other that Nick was coming, and doors remained firmly shut. Consequently, Nick was reduced to living in the caves near the rifle range at Kidderminster, or in railway huts. When things got really bad he would stagger home, shamefaced, to his mum. She would sober him up for a time, but then something else would happen, and he would fall off the wagon yet again, and repeat the cycle - but that cycle was an ever-downward spiral!

Singing the Blues

During one of Nick's intermittent sober periods Billy Reid, a famous English song-writer, was looking for a singer to showboat two new songs: one, *Make Your Manāna Today*, written for the Eurovision Song Contest. Vanessa Heath, Nick's agent and a mutual friend, recommended that Reid check out Nick, who was performing at a nightclub in Birmingham. Nick 'knocked 'em dead' on the night that Reid popped in. Reid was so impressed that he booked an orchestra and the studio of De Lane Lea in London for Nick to record his song. This was the big break Nick had been dreaming of.

Reid's reputation was such that, on entering the Contest, his song would have automatically jumped any preliminary rounds to appear on the final television show that was aired by the BBC. On that show, which would have an audience of over ten million, the viewers would vote for Britain's entrant, both song and singer, to the Contest. Since Reid didn't want to fail in front of such a huge audience, he decided to send Nick out on four club bookings in order to survey audience reactions, before finally deciding about submitting the song to the organisers. The first three shows went very well, and so Nick set off, full of confidence, to the final performance at the Playboy Club in London. He never got there. Nick woke up in the sea at Scarborough, togged out in full evening dress suit complete with dicky-bow, but now covered in sand and soaked in sea water.

Wandering aimlessly around the sea front, he was picked up by the police. Nick couldn't remember his name, or how he got to Yorkshire. To this day he still doesn't know how he made that two hundred mile journey. The police packed him off to the local hospital, and there he ended up in the psychiatric ward. That's where hopeless alcoholics were sent in those days. He was discharged after a detox, full of good intentions, but it wasn't long before he was back on the bottle.

Squaring the Vicious Circle

What a difference to today's Nick, who stresses the importance of an innate self-reliance, a pride in all he does, as well as a satisfaction in the achievements of all those around him. It is there for all to see in his sobriety, and in how he convinces other alcoholics to follow suit. It is there too in the way Chaucer is run. It is there in his insistence that, in order to recover, the addicts must first hit rock bottom, see themselves as pathetic, and understand why society treats them with contempt. From rock bottom the only way is up.

Alcoholism is an illness, and it must be accepted as such by each reforming drunk; but it is an illness that can, and must be overcome. Each drunk must really want to master his/her illness That desire, and the pride in the achievement of sobriety, can be powerfully reinforced by remembering all the guilt and shame. At the core of Nick's philosophy for renewal is the need to "recollect the monster you were, but are no more." Thinking back to the days of self-loathing can provide the will to escape the vicious circle of addiction.

However, according to Nick these memories must be approached not in despair, but with humour. For his is no morbid philosophy, with everyone sitting around in a circle feeling sorry for themselves. Nick always evokes the humour in his own life story, whether he is talking at Chaucer, to friends, or indeed when he and I were chatting about material for this book. The reason he tells these anecdotes is not just because he sees the constructive side of never forgetting his personal remorse. For he will never be tempted back to the brink of addiction. Nick doesn't need a hair shirt of dark memories to keep him on the straight and narrow.

By telling his stories, and inviting the 'members' of Chaucer to laugh, both at him and with him, he is saying it is OK for drunks to laugh at themselves. On my very first visit to Chaucer, my immediate impression was that there was laughter everywhere; I was expecting a very sombre and solemn place. Instead I saw Nick put into practice what he preaches: that everyone in the Clinic must laugh inwardly and outwardly at the people they were, but never forgetting that "it's only funny if you're not going to do it again."

The help and support of others is a fundamental part of any return to sobriety, particularly in the form of confidential one-to-one sessions. However, that support must be unsentimental, ruthless even, in helping drunks to help themselves. If those drunks are to avoid a return to degradation then the memory of the horrors must be kept fresh in their minds and continually confronted. Laughter prevents these memories, which will inevitably come back a-haunting, from being destructive. By not forgetting the uniqueness of their experiences, recovering alcoholics will stay within the virtuous circle of recovery, and not dive back into the vicious circle of alcohol abuse. Nick's message is one of rebuilding self-esteem and pride, by focusing on, and thereby transcending, any emotion of anger and frustration. So his sessions at Chaucer are not about fearfully indulging in morbid remembrances or wallowing in self-pity; they have the positive purpose of being part of the construction of a new future, and a pride in future success, but a purpose buttressed by the warnings of failures from the past.

However, Nick says there can be no inoculation against alcoholism: "Once an alcoholic, always an alcoholic. The trick is to want to stay sober, and to believe sincerely that it is a better way." The path to alcoholism is personal, as is the way back to sobriety. "We are all paddling our own canoe, only the drunk has to paddle upstream." The causes of each drunk's alcoholism are necessarily unique, which is why, in his clinic, Nick has set out to facilitate the self-recovery of each Chaucer 'member;' each recovery being an individual act of will.

No Magic Formula

The new Nick has learned these lessons the hard way. Having rediscovered the joy of living and a purpose in life, Nick knows it is good to be alive. That self-knowledge factors into all his priorities, both personal and professional. Consequently he totally rejects the idea that there can be some production line that feeds drunks in one end, and churns out valuable members of society from the other. The wannabe-sober drunk must be treated on his/her own merits, and not according to some list of rules that can only ever deal with symptoms, all the while ignoring the unique causes.

Hence, because of his very personal approach, for Nick there can be no dependency on repetitive formulae: no more leaning on lamp-posts. He has no time for methodolics, because he recognizes that mechanistic procedures, which promote a 'one-size fits all' support of recovery, come at a price; and that price is too high. Nick applauds any approach that leads to a strategic appreciation of the uniqueness in each situation. However, most of the approaches on offer elsewhere to the aspiring ex-drunk, and indeed those that failed Nick in his search for sobriety, smack of a production line.

There is an uncanny parallel between treating people in mechanistic ways and the so many popular business processes. Both bring with them the comfortable (and false) attractions of broad and vague generalisations that discount any inclusion of individual value and values in the process. Nick insists that such simplistic methodolic approaches are to be avoided like the plague. He sees dangerous similarities between the addiction of an alcoholic, and modern businesses' dependency on procedures that treat employees and customers as components in a mechanistic process. Both addictions leave those involved blinkered, obsessed with a single and misguided purpose of feeding their addiction, rather than playing a constructive role in their society.

Nick is dismayed by all addiction, be it chemically induced, or by exposure to business gurus with their procedural abstractions, checklists and the like. Both approaches give rise to addicts who have no conception of the uniqueness implicit in each particular situation. The same principles that underpin his treatment of alcoholics permeate his whole approach to the business of delivering that treatment. In his attitude I see a resonance with the words of Edmund Burke, the eighteenth century British Tory Politician who warned of the impact that industrial thinking would have on society: "Not men but measures: a sort of charm by which many people get loose from every honourable engagement." For Nick sees his engagement in business as the honourable development of a network of trust, which must be embraced as an involvement in personal relationships, and not avoided by hiding behind pseudo-intellectual mechanistic procedures. He puts his faith in his network, and insists that it cannot be automated and thereby replaced. His business, any business, simply cannot operate as if it is a depersonalised factory. Business must be about the celebration of personal values, not the lack of them camouflaged behind a list of rules and procedures.

That's no Lady, that's my Wife

Despite the importance Nick places on his memories, his recollections of this period of his life are inevitably patchy. Whole periods are completely blank, some are as clear as black and white, whereas others are psychedelic. He is nonplussed as he divulges that he managed to acquire two wives and a daughter during his days as a drunk. He married his first wife, Irene, in 1966, and the same year was delivered of a daughter, Tracey. However, his drinking was by now spiralling out of control, so much so that his poor wife could stand it no longer. Quite sensibly she threw him out of the house they had rented (or rather owed rent on), changed all the locks, and finally divorced him in 1971. Nick believes justice was done when "we split the house in half. Irene got the inside, and I got the outside."

When Nick looks back at his fourteen years on the booze, it fills him with a particular horror. He still wakes up in a cold sweat, thinking of how he casually led his innocent four-year old daughter into untold dangers. Nick was given weekend access, and she would spend those days in pubs or on park benches with her drunken dad, who would often leave her alone and unsupervised. Together they would spend time in the company of inebriates, and who-knows-what other type of degenerate.

On one occasion, with time to kill and no money, Nick, instead of leaving her, took her into a liquor store. "Are you going to pay for that bottle Dad?"
"What bottle?" he asked, dragging her quickly from the shop.
"The one you put in your pocket!"
"I don't know what you are talking about," Nick blustered.
"Did you borrow it, Dad?" No more was said.

She missed the next weekend to go to a family gathering. Nick was not invited, for obvious reasons. So the next time they met Nick asked: "did you enjoy meeting all your relations?" "I'd much rather go shoplifting with you Dad." Today's Nick is eternally grateful to Irene who, soon after this event, barred Nick from ever seeing his daughter again.

Nick married his second wife Carol during a particularly drunken period in 1973. They went their separate ways shortly after their wedding, following innumerable hysterical scenes. It was only when a sober Nick decided to marry Kelly in 1985 that he eventually started divorce proceedings. He has very little recollection of Carol. On one occasion he was shown a group photograph taken at that time, only to ask: "who is the pretty lady standing next to me?" It was only during the subsequent legal searches that Nick even became certain that he had actually married her, and that it wasn't all some alcohol induced nightmare.

Down and down, and yet further down. There were yet more psychiatric wards. However by now there were no more good intentions, no pretence following a detox: he went straight back to the next bottle. Nick was faced with a hand to mouth existence. So where would the next meal come from? More importantly where would the next drink come from? Nevertheless, even while on the booze, the entrepreneurial Nick was still hiding away in the background, straining to leap out. In fact Nick says that every drunk has to show entrepreneurial flare, albeit warped, on every single day of their drunken lives, just to find the food and (more importantly the) 'drink' to keep going.

By now Nick found himself on the streets of London, like so many drunks before and after him. He still had his guitar, and when 'gigs' were in short supply he would go busking, that is when he wasn't totally legless. In the summer Nick's patch was Tower Hill station, to catch the tourists, but he would retreat to Liverpool Street station whenever inclement weather struck. Even at his very lowest, a proud Nick refused to go begging, and so he always looked for innovative (?) alternatives.

One popular scam was to gatecrash weddings. Every Saturday there would be a big wedding reception being held somewhere in London. Nick would just turn up, and just take their food and drink. He would avoid meeting the bride and groom together, and as for everyone else he would tell the bride's side that he was a friend of the groom, and vice versa. What was the worst that could happen? On one occasion his ruse was discovered, and he was badly beaten and thrown into the canal!

Have a Drink on Me

Nick managed to find a job washing up and polishing glasses at a restaurant bar near the Square Mile that is London's financial district. The lunchtime clientele were always rushing back to work, leaving copious quantities of all sorts of alcoholic drinks behind: so-called 'seconds.' Nick didn't waste a drop. He bottled what he couldn't drink.

Over time many of the office workers and bankers who frequented the bar got to know him by name: even as a drunk he was still a raconteur. One evening, as he was enjoying a drink, Nick put one of his four bottles of 'seconds' scrounged that day on the counter, just to ease the weight in his overcoat pocket. A merchant banker, who nearly always bought him a drink, grabbed hold of the concoction and, holding it up to the light, exclaimed: 'That looks like a drop of the good stuff. What is it?'

Caught on the wrong foot, Nick's brain soon started working overtime. "An old friend of mine brews it; it's really amazing stuff." The top of the bottle was off now, and our posh friend began sniffing it expertly.

"Can I taste some?" The barman, a good friend of Nick's who resented the excessive affluence and patronizing behaviour of his clientele, 'cottoned on' to the situation. With a smirk he produced a clean spirit glass for the gentleman. A generous measure was poured and the banker raised the glass in the manner of a professional wine taster. "I say; this really is rather good. Do you think I could buy a bottle or two from you?"

Nick now got a little nervous. He could drink just about anything, and had regularly done so: adulterating cider with methylated spirits, and even rendering shoe polish, cough medicine, hair lacquer and after-shave. The after-shave had the extra benefit of making the drunk's usual dog-breath smell so much sweeter. Nick was immune to this rotgut, but he couldn't guarantee that it wouldn't do some serious damage to the City gent. However, the concern only lasted a split second. Even in his downward spiral, Nick the entrepreneur was never far from the surface. He heard his unscrupulous-self saying: "I paid one pound a bottle," quickly drowning out any residual qualms of conscience.

The banker decided to buy two bottles. If Nick could sell every bottle of seconds he made, then he could make some real money. Naturally, he would have to be careful when filtering the 'seconds.' He would ensure that the bottles were properly washed, and that none of the alcohol contained a mixer. Even so, the hygiene of this production line would have appalled any health inspector. The mixtures consisted of different wines, irrespective of colour, or whether they were sweet or dry. Sherry, port and quite often spirits were thrown in for good measure. Nick had no way of knowing the proof percentage of his product, but it all had quite a kick. Thanks to the money from satisfied customers, Nick could buy a steady supply of proper drink. The fad lasted quite a few weeks, in which time he could have poisoned half the office and banking population in and around Liverpool Street, but luckily he didn't hear of any complaints.

Santa's Blotto Grotto

Except for bar work, which is not a good idea for the aspiring alcoholic, casual jobs were few and far between, and getting scarcer. One particularly cold winter Nick was wandering aimlessly around a local department store, just keeping warm, when he became aware of the store's Santa Claus throwing his red hat at a very angry store manager. Santa, a 'resting' actor, had been offered a part in a pantomime at very short notice, and so he was off. The store manager was frantic: he had a long line of screaming children and irritable Mums waiting.

Nick said "I can do that!" and within ten minutes he was decked out in the red uniform, and encamped in his very own Grotto. To his delight he found that, apart from the stack of toys, Santa's Grotto was stocked with a dozen bottles of sherry. The booze was for the Mums to toast the festive season, while their little darlings received gifts from a ho-ho-ho-ing Nick. It wasn't long before this particular Saint Nick had drunk himself blotto. A demonic Old Nick told the mother of one screaming child to "take your s****y-a***d kid and chuck it in the f*****g river." If we are honest, we've all been tempted to do this at one time or another, but we've never had the courage. Nick, however, had imbibed sufficient courage, and so he found himself back on the streets again.

Sweet Dreams

Finding a place to sleep, particularly in winter, was the second most important task of the day: after finding booze. Shop doorways would do during the summer, although being hosed down with cold water every morning by the shopkeepers, who were washing away the mess in front of their premises, was always the downside. Thankfully, there was the ever-present support of the Salvation Army, and many nights Nick was grateful to sleep in a warm dormitory holding seventy plus vagrants, separated from his smelly neighbours by a mere eighteen inches between beds. However, there were really bad times when he would have to sit all night around the fire in the derelict Spitalfields market, sharing it with all the other dossers who were too disgusting even to be accepted into a hostel.

Nick also learned about the 'breakers-yard hotel' from some 'old-timers.' He would climb into a scrap yard at night, and curl up on the back seat of a wrecked car. The trick was to find one with the windows still intact, so as to avoid draughts. On one occasion, however, when all the wrecks were open to the elements, Nick made the almost fatal mistake of climbing into the boot of a wrecked Mercedes and closing the lid, before drinking himself snugly into oblivion.

He woke with a jolt after a very disturbed night. That was not really surprising, since as Nick opened the boot-lid he found his bed balanced precariously aboard a large car-transporter, now parked, thankfully for him, in the motorway service area of Leicester Forest East: a hundred and fifty miles from where he went to sleep! Nick hitchhiked back to London in a fury, where he screamed at the foreman of the yard. "I could have been killed. Don't you idiots check the cars before they're towed away?"

"We don't check any of the cars. Count yourself lucky mate. The Volvo next in line to your Merc' went into the crusher first thing this morning." Yet again Nick had somehow managed to slip through the clutches of the Grim Reaper.

The Sleep of the Dead

Another of Nick's favourite sleeping places during the summer was the local cemetery. He would snuggle down behind any large headstone that kept him out of the prevailing wind. Another trick, if it was raining, was to take the top stone off an ancient vaulted grave, nip inside, and pull the stone back into place, with a small space left for ventilation. He promised not to disturb the lead-lined coffin buried deep below, if it didn't disturb him.

It was on one such occasion, well after midnight and drunk with cheap rotgut, that Nick lay there restlessly tossing and turning. He just lay there with severe indigestion; not that he had eaten much. Hallucinating from the drink, and imagining all sorts of terrors, he saw lights flashing through the small breathing crack above his head. Ghosts? Vampires? Satanists? Body-snatchers? Terrified, he lay there, as silent as possible, hoping that the impending sinister presence would pass him by. His tormented stomach, however, would not obey his commands. Flatulence will out. The malodorous roll of thunder reverberating around inside the vault gave his location away.

There was nothing for it: he had to escape the approaching fiend. With superhuman strength he pushed the top stone aside and ran shrieking hysterically from the graveyard. Simultaneously, the policeman, who had been investigating a report of suspicious goings-on in the cemetery, dropped his flashlight and ran screaming in the opposite direction.

Of course, police cells always offered a nice warm place to sleep it off, often with breakfast thrown in. Nick was once dragged into Rochester Row police station on a drunk and disorderly charge. His possessions, including an almost full bottle of brandy, were taken off him and stuffed into a large envelope. This was sealed and Nick was asked to sign over the flap, before he was thrown in a cell for the night. As luck would have it the officer in charge of the cells was also a drunk: a situation not that uncommon in the police force.

By three o'clock in the morning Nick's bottle of brandy was preying on the officer's mind. All the while, Nick was shouting and screaming, 'effing and blinding,' in his cell. The cell door opened, and the officer entered, not to tell Nick to shut up, but to make him an offer he couldn't refuse. The policeman was holding Nick's property envelope. He would give Nick his bottle of brandy provided they could share it, and of course that Nick would sign over the flap of a new envelope containing his belongings minus the bottle. A deal! Side by side, both quietly drank themselves out of their mutual withdrawal agonies.

Harry the Hat

Finding a place to sleep in the winter was another matter. Nick spent many a night in the derelict Spitalfields Market around the legendary fire that was popular among the drunken skid-row tramps. (According to tramp mythology the fire had been burning unquenched for more than a century. The *London Evening Standard* reported that it was put out by the police in the mid-1970's only after several drunken tramps had fallen onto the embers and been severely burned.) Frozen to the bone, drunk on hair lacquer, and unable to sleep, he and his plastered pals would caterwaul through the night, convinced that their appalling singing was an equal of the Three Tenors. Nick remembers one particular night when Fred took off his shoes and socks to rub the circulation back into his feet, and one of his toes fell off. "I won't have to wash that one again!"

It was the same night that the word spread among the Spitalfields singers that Harry the Hat could take no more, and had decided to end it all. Shouting "I'm going to stop him. That b*****d owes me half a packet of fags," Nick rushed after Harry. Nick knew exactly where to go: the steps down to the Thames alongside London Bridge. But Harry was nowhere to be seen, although the Hat was slowly floating down the river. It wasn't long before Nick had returned to the fire, and was hitting the bottle yet again. Through tears of frustration at the futility of it all, he screamed at his companions "somebody's got to do something."

"Nobody cares," he was told.
"I bloody care."
"And what the hell can you do?"

Nick raged at the night: "I'll bloody well do something, I swear I will!" It would be some time before Nick was sober enough to keep his promise to the Hat.

Heaven can Wait

By now Nick was keeping company with 'pond life,' and in his alcoholic rages he would regularly upset some seriously evil people. On one occasion he woke to find the dosser next to him dead with his throat cut. Another time, a sixth sense had him hiding in a cupboard as a concrete paving slab was smashed down on his bed, exactly where his head had lain just minutes earlier. From time to time Nick had to get away from London. However, like every other alcoholic drifter, no matter what the dangers, he would never spend good drinking money on the buses and trains. 'Thumbing' lifts, or just walking were the only ways to get around. He was once dropped off in the middle of the countryside halfway through a 125-mile journey back to London.

Walking on in roughly the right direction he passed a lorry parked in a lay-by, un-laden except for a few sheets of polythene. He waited, hoping to catch the driver and ask for a lift, but there was no one to be seen, so he carried on.

A quarter of a mile further on, just before dusk, Nick came across a small village shop, and so he went in to try his luck. As usual his plan was to put some food in a shopping basket, and then theatrically discover at the checkout that his wallet had been stolen. His standard patter was that his broken-down car was being repaired, and if they would only lend him the money to buy some food he would return the cash immediately he got back home. Of course nobody ever believed him, although the odd charitable shopkeeper would sometimes take pity on him and give him the food. But not this one! "Had your wallet pinched? Shame. The world is full of crooks!" The shopkeeper did, however, condescend to a glass of water.

"Thanks a lot!"

While the shopkeeper's back was turned Nick pocketed a 'mini-stapler' from a display hook near the till, more out of malice than forethought. Outside, just as he was about to dump it in a waste bin, Nick's lateral logic connected the stapler with the polythene sheets he had seen earlier, and came up with a plan for a warm night's sleep. Backtracking, Nick was delighted to see the lorry still there, complete with polythene, and the driver nowhere to be seen. Dragging some sheets into a nearby field, Nick folded them to form a sleeping bag, just as he had been taught with blankets at the Boy Scout camps of his childhood. The stapler put the finishing touches to an immaculate bed. Nick's last recollection before descending into alcoholic unconsciousness was that the sky was looking extremely dark.

He awoke with a start some hours later, uncannily snug but totally disorientated. Nick had become aware of being bathed in a shimmering ethereal white light. "My God, I've died and gone to heaven." The initial mix of terror and release was soon elbowed out by a nagging question: "Do they have hangovers in heaven?" Tearing away at the staples, Nick emerged from his polythene shroud to find that it had snowed heavily during the night, and he was lying beneath a two-foot drift.

Then a strange and highly accented voice interrupted his reveries. "You may think you're in heaven lad, but as far as I'm concerned you're a bloody nuisance layin' there on my 'taters." Nick mumbled a few words to the local farmer, and then shuffled off towards London.

The Hound of the Baskervilles?

During his formative years, his relations were always telling Nick that he was a direct descendent of one of England's oldest families: the Herefordshire Baskervilles. What could be more natural, during one of his major binges, than to go down to Herefordshire and reclaim his birthright? Staggering around the county, he would tell the sad story to anyone who would listen. He made a nuisance of himself the length and breadth of the shire. Arrested on more than one occasion, Nick told and re-told his story to Sergeant James, the very patient desk sergeant at the small police station serving the area around the Baskerville ancestral home.

Unbeknownst to Nick, just twenty miles away, a most heinous crime was being committed: the kidnap, rape and murder of a young woman. The police had issued a description of the perpetrator, whom the press had labelled the Black Panther. By now the reader will not be surprised to hear that the 'photo-fit' bore a close resemblance to Nick.

Meanwhile, in a drunken haze, he was stumbling along country back-roads, looking for somewhere to crash. He came across a small one-man garage business, where the proprietor was servicing a fleet of six elderly coaches. Nick explained that his Jaguar had broken down. He was returning from a visit from London where he had visited his daughter, who had been separated from him by his divorce. Very pleased with his story, Nick then asked if he could sleep in one of the coaches for a couple of hours. The man agreed instantly, even offering Nick a cup of tea. Convinced that the man had been taken in by his eloquence, Nick settled down on the back seat of the coach for a long, comfy and contented kip.

Nick was totally unaware of the manhunt underway in the vicinity, but the garage owner wasn't. Thinking that he had trapped the villain, he immediately called the police. It wasn't long before a terrifying roar shattered Nick's sleep. The first thing that came into focus was half a dozen police officers, each brandishing a sinister looking handgun, all pointing at his head. A melee of shouting and screaming ensued, just like in the American cop movies. He was searched, trussed up like a chicken, and finally thrown into the back of a Black Maria police van.

Twenty minutes later Nick was sat in the now familiar interview room, facing a very intimidating Sergeant James, who was somewhat doubtful that his colleagues had caught the right man. Nevertheless the policeman asked: "What do you have to say for yourself. Did you think you could get away with kidnapping and demanding a bloody ransom?" The desk sergeant and his colleagues were very surprised when Nick responded: "I've got to tell you something!" The veins stood out in a perplexed Sergeant James's neck, and beads of perspiration ran down his face. The room fell silent, as all the officers leaned forward, straining to hear the confession. Nick stood there trembling, and was having real trouble finding the words. They spilled out abruptly: "I've messed my pants."

The arresting officer lost his patience, and the furious sergeant lost the plot: "Throw him in the cells, but first get him cleaned up!" Nick was confined in the only lavatory in the police station, together with sufficient toilet paper, soap, water and a towel. Locking himself in, Nick was about to start his ablutions when he noticed a tiny window above his head, just big enough for a child to crawl through - a child or a malnourished alcoholic! The lavatory was on the ground floor, so Nick calculated that he had at most six or seven feet to fall. It was a very tight squeeze, but somehow he made it.

However, and with Nick there is always an however, he had no way of knowing that the police station was situated next to a dairy farm. Nor did he know that such establishments always housed a tank, capable of holding hundreds of gallons of waste milk, often to a depth of over six feet. Even if he had known, he would never have suspected that such a tank would be located directly under the window from which he was making his escape!

His half-starved body left the tiny window with a plop, and a fraction of a second later he hit the disgusting mass of rotting milk and cream below. He barely managed to drag himself half-drowned and squelching from the tank. He'd had enough. Nick struggled back around to the front door and knocked with what remained of his strength, standing there just like a B-movie "Monster from the Black Lagoon."

Driven to distraction, Sergeant James let out: "What the f***!!" By now, of course, his colleagues had come to realise, what the desk sergeant had already suspected, that Nick was no kidnapper. They had gone to release Nick, but had found the door locked from the inside. Looking through the peephole in the door they just caught sight of Nick's feet disappearing through the window. They were silently very relieved to find that he had absconded; it avoided embarrassing questions about the police going off on a wild goose chase while the real culprit was still at large. Therefore the sergeant was not at all pleased to find this pathetic and pitiful apparition re-fouling his station steps, and smelling even more disgusting than last time.

"I broke out, but I want to come back!" The cop-shop door slammed shut in Nick's face. Slowly he walked away through the early evening gloom, one painful, tortuous step at a time, the vile liquid soaking him slowly to the bone. The smell was indescribable. Every breath caused him to vomit, and by now the cold had started his teeth chattering. Half a mile, and almost an hour later, he caught sight of a shed, overgrown with vegetation. Nick forced his way inside, and sank to the floor, to rest and take stock. The smell was worse than ever.

As his eyes became accustomed to the gloom, he noticed a little light filtering through a filthy window covered in dirt, dust and cobwebs. Suddenly the moon came out from behind a cloud, and through the window Nick saw the back gardens of a small row of houses. Not thirty feet away was the answer to his prayers, a washing line full of shirts, socks, towels, a couple of pairs of jeans, and less importantly to Nick a dozen pairs of ladies knickers. He removed his evil-smelling clothes and scraped his body clean of the rancid cream, and stark naked, but with renewed vigour, he left his refuge. Quickly over a two-foot high garden fence, he crept stealthily up to the washing line. Towelling himself down, he carefully chose a shirt, and then walked through the knickers towards a suitable pair of jeans.

What Nick didn't know was that the locality had been terrorised for many months by a mysterious 'knicker nicker.' He had blundered into a deliberate trap set to catch the pervert. Suddenly the area was lit up as bright as day by the powerful beams from several police flashlights. For the second time that day, although this time naked, Nick was pinned to the ground by the long arm of the law. On this occasion, however, he had the extra concern that a newly awakened hate mob of knickerless neighbours was also screaming for his blood.

The arresting officer, jubilant to have finally got his man, dragged Nick back to the police station, only to have the smile wiped from his face as he confronted a very angry Sergeant James. Thanks to Nick the only lavatory in the station was now situated behind a door locked from the inside. The unrelieved sergeant was bursting, and so he barred the door on Nick. "I couldn't care if your f*****g family owns the whole of Herefordshire. You will never darken my door again. Do you hear me? Never, ever set foot in MY county again! Now piss off."

There was nothing for it, but to rejoin the degenerate underclass back in London.

4

Lost among the Bottom Feeders

When Nick and I were considering what exactly to include in this book, and particularly how to tell Nick's life story, the usual form of our discussions was for me to mention certain sacred cows of management, and then to wait for Nick's spontaneous reaction. My recounting of such "management bulls**t" normally led to a great deal of incredulous laughter on Nick's part, not to say total disbelief, quickly followed up with a stream of anecdotes he considered relevant.

Nick's natural scepticism verged on cynicism the first time I told him about the perennial favourites of management courses: Ethics and Culture. "When I hear the word culture, I slip back the safety catch of my revolver" (Hanns Johst).

"And as for Ethics," he lisped, "that's an Inglith county to the eath't of London!" (For non-British readers the county to the east of London is Essex.) The problem with the study of ethics is that, perversely, it can supply the weasel words used to justify the very behaviour it sets out to question. Unethical behaviour, however well or badly it is justified, is still an act of personal choice. "There is a huge gulf between knowing what is wrong, and choosing not to do wrong, or even caring about it: ask any drunk!"

As far as Nick is concerned it's the same with choices made by management. In the unavoidable stress of a particularly diabolical management panic, an act of choice can start uneventfully, unwittingly, with a series of tiny transgressions, each seeming so obvious and harmless, beneficial even. Such are the first tentative steps along this primrose path, this one-way street to perdition. There are no alarm bells; life goes on, only with each infringement the choices become just that little bit more corrupt and corrupting: drip, drip, drip, until the floodgates open. The parallel with the decline into the degeneracy of alcoholism is there for all to see.

Both ENRON and their auditors Andersen, as well as WorldCom and all the others, were stuffed to the brim with MBAs, many of who had been taught ethics. However, under the twin onslaughts of market-led pressures and personal ambitions, did that make any difference to the choices made? There's no need to answer that hypothetical question! Would John De Lorean, overdosing on ethics, have been entrapped with packets of cocaine in his futile attempt to save his floundering motor company? No doubt in all these cases, the managers' responses were: "Deeds must, when the devil drives." No one in all of these ethically-aware (or otherwise) managements had learned the important lesson that "when you sup with the devil, use a long spoon!"

The Ultimate Unethical Business Choice
Down, and down, and down you go, until eventually you hit rock bottom, and there you will find a whole new social ecology among the low life, and the criminals who feed on them. "Crime is just the ultimate unethical business choice." Nick speaks from experience, having met many criminals in his travels: as we shall soon see. The values of polite society simply have no bearing there. For this is where the real meaning of culture, "the way we do things here," can be seen as "nature, red in tooth and claw." Cut loose from normal social constraints, both the failing manager and the drunk soon find out exactly what immorality and extreme violence so-called humanity is capable of.

Culture isn't artificially created by some diktat from on high, some purpose of the powerful. It is the sum total of the sponta-neous behaviours and hypocrisies of everyone involved, their knee-jerk reactions, their true selves, independent of any namby-pamby moralising or strategising by so-called thought-leaders. An understanding of culture doesn't come from the wish lists of sanitised textbooks, but from observing the social stabilities and rituals that emerge from the natural selection amongst both the basest and the highest motives across society.

Even among the cascade of unethical behaviour, driven by the most vicious excesses of greed, and in the hopelessness of despair, down among the 'pond life,' it is still possible to find kindness, generosity and friendship. But not a lot! People down on their luck will bond, in the hope that they will uncover some form of synergy that will be of mutual advantage. Thus it was when Nick met Jeff, his pal and soon to be 'partner in crime,' in the Salvation Army canteen. Nick swapped an egg for Jeff's thin sausage. They had so much in common ... both were musicians and both alcoholics! They even looked alike and could be mistaken for brothers. However, as with all addicts, their friendship proved to be worth no more than the price of the next fix. But Nick wouldn't discover this fact until much later.

Gon' Fishin'

On one of their first adventures together, Jeff and Nick were strolling along the Grand Union Canal, on the look out for booze, up to no good as usual. On the opposite bank they spotted an angler, patiently dangling his bait in the water, a six-pack propped up invitingly at his side.

How could they distract him and get away with the booze? Nick had the answer. Jeff would jump into the canal a little way upstream, and splash around pretending to be drowning. When the rescuer reached the spot, Nick would have it away with the cans. Jeff wasn't so sure; he couldn't swim. Silver-tongued Nick convinced him that the canal was only a couple of feet deep; after all canal boats are flat bottomed because the water is so shallow.

Jeff jumped into six foot plus of muddy filthy canal; he didn't need to pretend about drowning. The fisherman didn't move; despite the screams he just stood there, still as a statue, intent on watching the end of his line. Panicking, Nick rushed past, dived in and dragged Jeff out. Both were now covered in muck and slime. Cursing and swearing they staggered back along the canal bank to remonstrate with the angler, only to notice a hearing-aid poking out of his left ear. He was deaf, and to make things worse, our heroes looked down to see a six-pack of ... alcohol-free lager.

Criminal Masterminds

In his fourth year of vagrancy, when he was still a loner, Nick was to experience a situation that epitomises the futility and hopeless-ness of the homeless drunk. A sympathetic proprietor of a local taxi company had offered him a bunk bed in a recess in the ceiling above, and out of sight of, the control-centre microphone desk. Each night he would climb up a ladder to bed, only to be fumigated out of his hideout before six in the morning by the chain-smokers starting the morning shift below. Then Nick would walk the streets until he could find a pub open. Even in generosity, a vicious circle was well and truly operational.

This was how Nick first came across a certain notorious public house in the East End of London, run by a local gang boss. However, these small-time crooks were no criminal masterminds; they wouldn't graduate to the big league for quite some time to come. The first time Nick went to the pub, it was to return 'empties.' By then he had met up with his friend Jeff, and together they were paid tuppence for each bottle. The barman stacked the empties in a crate, and dumped them out the back. The backyard was not locked, so our heroes simply picked up the bottles, entered the pub through the front door, and received yet more money. They pulled this stunt half a dozen times before they were eventually 'sussed,' and that only happened because the pair decided to loiter at the bar for a drink.

A Life on the Ocean Wave

Not for the last time did Nick merit the displeasure of this violent band of malefactors. On one occasion he can vaguely remember that the gang bosses had put a price on his head - valuing his life as high as the price of a crate of light ales. He had to skip town: he would run away to sea!

He set off, already drunk, for what he thought was the East India Docks, planning to stowaway on a foreign-bound ship, with just a few bottles for company. Nick was surprised at just how easily he got aboard his chosen ship, a sturdy looking vessel. He climbed into a narrow broom cupboard, and passed out. When he finally came around Nick began to suspect that the ship was having engine trouble, because it kept stopping and starting.

He had planned to hide for a week, but he was withdrawing from the booze, and was in a very poor state of health. After two days, and feeling dreadful, he dragged himself out from the cupboard; his supply of booze had run out. Nick decided it was time to hand himself over to the captain. He would work his passage; perhaps he could even get a job as a barman. His admission came as quite a surprise to the captain of the Woolwich Ferry. For while Nick had been drinking himself silly, and subsequently sobering up and suffering withdrawal symptoms, he had been crossing, back and fore, from one bank of the River Thames to the other.

Honour Among Thieves?

News of his river crossings eventually reached the gang bosses. They laughed themselves silly, and so he was quickly forgiven. Nick's real life experience became so well known that comedians on the club circuit turned it into one of their standard jokes.

Soon Nick settled back among this band of villains, where he was to experience at first-hand an alternative sub-culture ('sub-' being the operative word), devoid of the hypocrisy prevalent in polite society. Here he learned very quickly that there is no 'honour among thieves,' although he was to observe a perverse, yet nonetheless consistent logic.

It was not uncommon for one gang member to enjoy the 'company' of the wife or girlfriend of another in the crew. On one particular occasion, the dalliance was discovered. The cuckolded husband arranged for two thugs to go around to his own house and beat up his wife (his wife note, and not the fellow gang member!) Eventually the husband returned home, where he found his wife lying bloodied and unconscious on the kitchen floor. He was incandescent with rage, and immediately called up the services of yet more thugs to 'sort out' the original two.

When he returned to the pub in order to manufacture an alibi for the second attack, he was met with total disbelief from his fellow drinkers, who were at a loss over his motives. "What are you up to? It was you who paid them to do the 'job' in the first place."

"I was furious with those f*****g idiots. They should've waited until she'd cooked my supper."

Gold-finger

There was certainly no sense of honour toward other criminal gangs. The gang at the pub had heard rumours of a safety deposit box, owned by another crook, which was stuffed full of money: a soft target. He could hardly complain to the police! The raid took place, and the gang got clean away with all the loot. But they were not a happy bunch; there was only six pounds in cash.

Granted there were half a dozen solid gold bars, worth tens of thousands of pounds: but only six quid! Not very bright, these gangsters! We must remember that at the time they were just a bunch of local tearaways, who hadn't the slightest idea of how to 'fence' their big league booty. This was just the start of their journey along the learning curve. Ten years on the same gang would have no trouble in placing their loot.

However, one particularly gifted gang member did come up with a novel use for his gold bar. He was getting married soon, and needed to buy wedding rings. So he did what seemed eminently sensible to him, and took his ingot to a local jeweller's shop. "Sir needs to bring the required amount of gold for the rings. We cannot possibly accept the responsibility of a bar of solid gold."

"'Aven't you got an 'acksaw out the back?"

"Sir, we are jewellers, not ironmongers," came the reproof. The gangster, true to his roots, rushed back to the pub, and sure enough he managed to unearth a saw. With a huge chunk of gold hacked off one corner, he returned. "Is Sir marrying an elephant?" Pleased with his joke, the jeweller, of course, knew better than to inform the police.

The gang member told all his mates the story, and not surprisingly he became known as Goldfinger. Many other English gangsters since have taken on this sobriquet, particularly the big-time criminals involved in the 1983 Brinks Mat robbery when 6800 bars of gold were stolen: but ours was the first to take on the name of the James Bond villain.

It served him well, for as he started out on a stretch at her Majesty's Pleasure in Wormwood Scrubs Prison (now that really is a culture!), his reputation as a gold robber preceded him. He was considered to be a Mr Big, which ensured respect from inmates and guards alike. Little did they know that in those days he was in reality a 'Fools Gold'-finger.

The Reluctant Bank Robber

These were the people that Nick rubbed shoulders with on his daily pub-crawl. Sometimes he supplemented his rapidly receding entertainment earnings by working as lunchtime barman at their pub; it brought a few drinks and an extra quid or two.

The gang knew Nick as a 'rock and roll' singer. Usually by one o'clock in the afternoon most, if not all, of the gang members were present, together with numerous hangers-on. Often Nick would be asked to entertain them with an 'evening' rock session. Basically the gang kept him around because he could play the guitar and sing, even though increasingly he was becoming a drunken liability.

But he was always there, with a joke, a smile, and a song. In a short space of time Nick was considered 'on their firm,' although at the time he was not entirely sure what this meant. But he was about to find out. An incident took place at the beginning of the summer, which in hindsight should have given him pause for thought, and should perhaps have caused him to reconsider his risky position. The reality, of course, was that the only matter to receive any serious consideration by Nick was where the next drink was coming from.

The gang had planned a bank robbery, but it was "all going pear-shaped." The final straw for the Big Boss was when the getaway driver phoned to say he had tripped and broke an ankle. In desperation, the Boss turned to Nick, "can you drive?"

Bemused, Nick nodded. "Right, the car's outside; take us down the bank." Mr Big was tight lipped, and although Nick was inebriated, he was rightly terrified of the gangster, and left with absolutely no choice. The Boss had solved his immediate problem, but once again Mr Big showed that he wasn't that substantial in the personnel department.

Not being in on the planning, the shanghaied Nick had no idea what was happening, or the implications. He has only a very blurred recollection of the first part of the trip. After his passengers had entered the bank, a beaming Nick too got out of the car, and stood proudly beside the Mk.9 Jaguar telling passers-by about 'his' wonderful motor.

Meanwhile the crooks' run of bad luck continued. Someone had informed on them! The police were lying in wait, and all of the gang were promptly arrested ... except for a bemused Nick. He was watching open-mouthed from the opposite side of the road.
Only then did it dawn on Nick what was happening. The first thought to come to his befuddled mind was that the gang would think he was the 'grass' (the informant) who turned them in to the law, even though until that very moment he had no idea what was going down. He was as good as dead - unless he too was arrested. Jail was a lot better than being murdered!

Still half-cut, Nick looked frantically around and recognised one of the arresting officers. He was a police sergeant, a decent man, who would arrest Nick for being drunk and disorderly at least twice a week - every week. Not unreasonably, the sergeant considered him to be a complete and utter nuisance. Nick staggered over to the officer, addressing him by name, all the while holding his hands in the air. Turning around to face Nick, the policeman snapped: "What do you want?"

"Sergeant Campbell, sir, I'm the getaway driver," stuttered the hapless Nick.

"And I'm the policeman telling you to ... Piss Off," said the sensible Campbell. No self-respecting criminal would ever use a drunk like Nick Charles as a getaway driver.

Needing no second bidding, Nick ran off, back to the pub. The landlord listened to the sorry tale, and at the end enquired of the whereabouts of his car. Nick said he had left it behind. "Go get it you dick 'ead," roared the landlord. Nick crept back to the bank, coat collar turned up, furtively looking in every direction. The police were gone, the bandits too, as well as all the onlookers. The Jaguar was exactly where he had left it, keys still in the ignition. So Nick got in, and quietly drove away.

He tried three more times to give himself up, all to no avail. "For the last time, there was no car in the hold-up. Do you think we're idiots. You're not going to scrounge free bed and board out of the legal system. Just go away!" It didn't take long for the gang to figure out that real 'grass' was the original getaway driver, with the broken ankle. Nick didn't have to leave town after all.

Call Me Madam

It was around this time that Nick and Jeff entered the social circle of Tamara Hansen, an infamous East-End Madam: purveyor of attractive young ladies to the rich and famous. In her line of business good administrative help is hard to find, otherwise she would never have used Nick and Jeff as gophers. They would run messages, and it was their job to stuff phone boxes in London's West End with cards advertising the girls' services, and strip out the cards of any competition.

This was a never-ending job - for apart from the competition returning the favour, the phone company would regularly clear out all the sordid promotional material from their boxes. One day, tired of this merry-go-round, Jeff proudly told Tamara that he had solved the problem: "Easy, I took their cards down, I put ours up, and then I super-glued the doors of the phone boxes shut."

One day Tamara sent Jeff to get condoms from the local hairdressers. He was unaware of a long-standing bulk order supplied once a month at a discount rate, and instead returned with a few 'packs of three.' Tamara was less than pleased. "How long do you think that will last? Militant Millie uses more on her week-end off." Jeff slunk away muttering under his breath: "They'd last me for months." He eventually returned puffing and panting with several carrier bags.

On another occasion Tamara was throwing a 'Schoolgirls and Vicars' party, so she sent Jeff to buy two-dozen pairs of navy blue school knickers. She warned him to make sure that some were big enough to fit Fat Alice, one of Tamara's more popular girls. Unsure, but not daring to go back to Tamara, he asked Nick what sizes he should look for. He was told: "If they fit you, they'll fit Alice." Some hours later, Tamara received a call from Rochester Row police station to say that Jeff was being held in custody. He had been arrested in the changing room at the C&A department store in Oxford Street trying on schoolgirl's knickers.

Tamara's main indulgence was her prize greyhounds. Nick and Jeff were given the job of exercising them, and were paid well for their efforts. She would have been horrified had she known the dogs spent most of their 'walkies' sat in a pub a mile away. One extremely gifted runner, who had won many races, suddenly became an also-ran. Tamara became suspicious, and she arranged for someone to follow our heroes on an early evening exercise walk. He reported back that Nick and Jeff had popped into a 'take-away' for three donner kebabs, one each for our heroes and one for the dogs to share. Our dynamic duo had to stay away from the 'manor' for well over a week until Tamara had calmed down.

A Private Member

On the odd occasion, the pair would drive 'the girls' to their assig-nations. But it was only the odd occasion, because Tamara was an extremely shrewd lady, and very wary of the drunks ability to deliver 'the goods.' However, one time she was desperate. One of her girls, Sexy Susie, had a rendezvous with a Member of Parliament: let's call him Humphrey. Humphrey's particular fancy was for al fresco sex; he loved to go out into the countryside, and "have it away in a field."

Naively Nick had believed that his adopted underworld culture was separate from, and preyed on proper society. Of course he had met many important people before, but they were drunks en route to the scrap heap where Nick himself lived. So it came as a great shock to see high officers of the state symbiotically co-existing with criminals. He has never forgotten this first lesson on how hypocrisy camouflages the dark side of every culture.

Nevertheless, money is money, and that money buys booze. Therefore, whatever Humphrey wants, Humphrey gets! Jeff was the chosen driver. He was to drive the couple out along the Whitechapel Road, Bow Road, through Stratford and onto the main Southend arterial road, towards a field that had previously been identified as suitable for the occasion. Susie and Humphrey were to strip off, leave their clothes in the car, and saunter off to play. This left Jeff on guard.

Bored, parked next to a phone-box in the lay-by, what does every drunkard do? Drink of course! He had brought along a bottle of Irish whiskey, bought with his earnings from this evening's work. Very soon Jeff was in no state to notice the police car rolling up alongside. Finding him in a stupor, the officers decided that one of them would drive Jeff back to the cells for the night, and the other would follow in Jeff's car; the clothes of Susie and Humphrey still scattered over the back seat.

Some time later Tamara received a frantic 'collect call' from Susie. Tamara swung into action. She phoned the pub, and demanded that Nick stop his act. He must go immediately to fetch the pair of 'lovebirds,' who by now were shivering in the dark lay-by.

Nobody in the pub argued; nobody dared argue with Tamara. She was one tough lady. In a frantic rush to comply with her demands, the gang almost threw Nick through the door.

Nick ran around to Tamara's place to pick up a car, where he mistakenly inquired, "how will I recognise them?" "Just how many f*****g bare-arsed politicians d'y think you're gonna find on the Southend Road?" The behaviour of such politicians, whether bare-arsed, or bare faced, raise many more interesting questions about both ethics and culture, but we have to leave that, and return to our world of alternative behaviour.

Caravan Holiday

At that time Jeff was living in a derelict caravan owned by Tamara, and parked on some waste ground behind one of her properties. Tamara had allowed Jeff to live there, provided he renovated it. For a smart lady, she did make some truly crazy decisions. One of the daftest was the time she went away for a long weekend, leaving Jeff and Nick in charge of her business.

Jeff decided he would take advantage. What did Tamara expect? The only thing you can rely on with drunks is that they are unreliable! He would ask the next customer with a particularly exotic request for double the normal rate. According to Jeff's thinking the punter was unlikely to complain, and he, Jeff, would pay Tamara the correct amount, pocket the difference and spend it on booze.

Sure enough, a client phoned in, asking about having sex on Kensington High Street! The extra price was fixed, and Jeff left Nick to work out the details. The caravan immediately came to mind. Our heroes invested in a new set of tyres, attached the caravan to Tamara's car, and with both Rusty and her client comfortably settled in the van, they headed off to Kensington.

Jeff parked the caravan, and as it bounced frantically up and down on it's worn-out suspension, he and Nick sat patiently in the car, keeping a look out.

Nick suddenly spotted a policeman hurrying towards them. Jeff, in the driver's seat, slammed the car into gear, and screeched away. The sudden acceleration came as a great shock to the rusting thirty-year old caravan. So much so, that the undercarriage separated from the superstructure. Nick and Jeff careered off with just the chassis in tow. Meanwhile the bodywork of the trailer came crashing to the ground; it crumpled like a concertina. The structural shock to the van was as nothing compared to that experienced by coupling couple inside; but Nick and his pal weren't hanging around to find out what happened next.

The policeman was too busy laughing to worry about the couple that staggered partially clothed from the van. Taking advantage of the confusion, a street-wise Rusty helped her friend to slip away, leaving the van with no identifying features littering up the High Street. No doubt Rusty got a bonus for facilitating the escape.

The Last Chance Saloon

Nick had realised that this life-style couldn't go on indefinitely. But try as he may, his periods of sobriety, when he would start to rebuild his life, would be followed by a binge taking him back down to the bottom. On one occasion he managed to stay sober from January to October 1976.

He even held down an evening job as a waiter in the Garrick Club in London, a time he looks back on with great affection, and gratitude towards the staff, management and members. During the day, he also worked as a barman at The Barley Mow in Westminster. He managed to resist the booze despite working behind a bar.

At last he felt he was over the booze and so he decided to telephone his mother with the good news that he had rejoined the human race. His father answered with the news that Nick's mother had died on Christmas Eve 1975. Devastated he went up to see the grave, and immediately "went back on the piss again."

The binge lasted six weeks, and he woke up in a squat in Wandsworth, where an evil monster threatened to cut his head off. That was it. He caught a bus back into the city, to The Barley Mow, where despite having disappeared for six weeks, he hoped they would take him back onto the staff.

Needing some 'Dutch courage' to face the imminent interrogation, Nick first popped into the Marquis of Granby for a 'quick one.' There, on 13th December 1976, half an hour before noon, Nick took his last alcoholic drink. He got the job at the Barley Mow, and despite being surrounded by booze, never again did he succumb to the demon drink.

5

The Northern Club Circuit

This time, after so many false starts, Nick really did have the inner strength to give up the booze. However, if he had problems when he was drinking, they were nothing compared to those he faced as he rejoined society. At least as a drunk his craving for booze superseded any worries about his social degradation. When he was a drunk he would stagger every day from the hostel near Liverpool Street Station all the way to Trafalgar Square, where he would meet up with his fellow drunks. Now he was sober, walking head held high, he was totally lost. As a drunk he never looked higher than four foot above the ground; sober he had to walk, head bowed, to remember his way around London.

As an ex-drunk he now re-entered a world where many of his old friends and family had given up on him long ago, and even those that remained were suspicious of being used yet again. He had been anaesthetised for 14 years, and had woken up to find the world was a shocking place; he was 32 years old, but thinking like an eighteen year-old. He had lost 14 years, and was amazed to find a shampoo and set no longer cost five shillings. In fact there weren't even shillings any more; decimalisation of the British currency had taken place in 1971 without him.

What was he to do? He had two choices. Carry on working in bars, a job he knew all too well; or entertain. Most of his show business contacts had rejected him years ago, so he had to build new relationships in the entertainment industry. Casual bar work in the Barley Mow public house in Horseferry Road brought in sufficient money to keep the wolf from Nick's door, as he travelled around the clubs of London gathering together a group of likely musicians: the Innovations. This had the unexpected side-benefit that the mother of the group's lead guitarist offered to rent him a room in the family home in Albatross Street, Plumstead.

A not-so Standard Lamp

As he was scouring the pubs and clubs looking for musical talent, his attention was drawn to table-lamps made out of (empty) Guinness bottles that were supplied to publicans by the Dublin company's marketing department. The only design problem with the product was that it had an electric cable trailing from its base, which made it unsuitable for use on tables in the centre of a room and away from wall-mounted electric sockets. Nick thought that the design would also be greatly improved if the lamp could be free standing, and with the bulb fitted inside the bottle. After much research he eventually tracked down battery-operated units small enough to fit inside the bottle: remember this was the 'seventies, and widespread electronic miniaturisation was still a decade away.

The wholesaler had 500 units; Nick bought the lot. He had created a handsome merchandising product suitable for any bottle. Just twist the top of the bottle, and lo and behold the light turned on. Nick sent the idea away to major manufacturers, but he was a man in a hurry. While waiting for their response he started offering prototypes to the publicans he knew, and many snapped up the novelty. Unfortunately there was a fatal design flaw. When the device had been running for more than 10 minutes ... it exploded - on one occasion within earshot! A still sober Nick scrapped the idea, and yet again he decided to leave town!

On the Street Where You Live

During his many lost years, Nick had no exposure to pop music, and so he had no knowledge of current trends. Consequently the Innovations played nostalgia rock music: 'sixties revival before revival was in vogue; once more he was ahead of his time. The group soon found that there were few takers for their particular brand of rock, and so they decided to change tack. They would try ... melody! That required a good female lead singer, and so they advertised in the music press. Kelly Miller turned up for the audition, and as they say, the rest is history. However, to hear Kelly tell the story, Nick and her were predestined to be together. Their paths had crossed three times previously. The first, when she was a very young passenger on the cruise ship SS Lakonia. She still has a vivid recollection of one particular private concert on board ship, where she found herself very taken with the young man who sang a yodelling number in the show - you guessed it: Nick!

Years later Nick spent one summer dossing in a garden shed on the street where she lived - Aldbourne Road, Acton; not quite a reprise of the storyline from My Fair Lady. Later still, Nick, while living in a hostel, saw Kelly appear on the New Faces television talent show. He was entranced, and even sent her, care of the show, a copy of a song he had written. Nick had remembered seeing her several times on television shows like *Z-Cars*, *Dixon of Dock Green*, *Black Beauty*, *Beryl's Lot* and in the film *Moon over the Alley*. Nick has subsequently discovered that when, during his married days in Worcestershire, he used to bounce his young daughter Tracey on his knee, he was accompanied by the children's hit song *Soldier, Soldier will you Marry Me*, sung by TV and radio personality Ed 'Stewpot' Stewart, and ... Kelly!

And now, here she was turning up to his audition. It was fate. They got on 'like a house on fire,' and very soon he and Kelly became an 'item.' Much to the annoyance of the rest of the band, he and Kelly also started a show within a show. They would joke with the audiences, inadvertently forming the basis of what would later become their cabaret act. Their ad hoc comedy routines used to go down so much better with the audiences than the rest of the group's performance. Very quickly the pair realised that their future in show business lay in cabaret; and the increasingly resentful band had now become a liability. The die was cast when they made the fateful decision to set out as a duo on the Northern Club circuit.

It wasn't long before their landlady gave Nick and Kelly notice to quit. With her son's dream of fame and fortune in pop music lying in tatters, her daughter-in-law stormed into the house and demanded that the duo were given their marching orders. Nick and Kelly quickly found a rented room with the Sharmas, an Asian family in Berkeley Avenue, Cranford, near to Heathrow Airport. Unfortunately it took money to buy costumes and equipment for their act, and so they had to find jobs, any jobs, before they could launch themselves on the club circuit. Nick ended up as a driver for National Car Parks (NCP), ferrying customers between the Excelsior Hotel and the airport terminals. Kelly became a cleaner at the Heathrow Hotel - quite a comedown from her glory days as a successful child actress.

Fish'n Chips

One day Nick was sent to Heathrow airport to meet a Dave Ellis arriving off a British Airways flight from Saudi Arabia. It turned out that Dave ran a haulage business based in Colnbrook, Middlesex. However, while driving a lorry in Saudi Arabia he was innocently involved in a fatal accident with a Saudi national. His articulated lorry was confiscated and he was thrown into prison, where he lived for nearly six months on rice and weevils, until the appropriate 'blood money' had been paid.

Dave's first words on seeing Nick holding his name aloft in the bustling arrival hall of Terminal Four was, "no arguments, take me to a fish and chip shop."
"But I was told to take you to..."
"Take me to a fish and chip shop!" Dave insisted.

He gorged his first real meal for six months without pausing for breath, and then demanded a pizza. Then he was sick; then he ate more; then he was sick again, and finally he fell asleep. Nick drove him home, and they have been friends ever since. In fact Dave became Chairman of the Trustees for Chaucer.

Much of Dave's business was with the Indian community in and around Southall. He was heavily involved with the 'Indi,' their self-help charitable organisation. Its main aim was to assist aspiring entrepreneurs in setting up businesses, so that they would go on to employ others, hopefully from among their own community. Dave introduced Nick and Kelly to the Indi, and members soon fixed them up with a rented house, a car, PA system, guitar and amplifier.

With their financial history, Nick and Kelly were in no position to arrange a loan for these items from a high street bank. The Indi fixed the required cash advance, and arranged the repayment of the capital sum on easy terms to three different local businessmen, one of whom was Dave Ellis.
Nick and Kelly now had their new musical equipment, a two-

year-old Alpha Romeo from Dave's garage, and an end of terrace house in Hounslow, which they were able buy just four years later having paid off all their other debts. Rehearsals began almost immediately, although Nick will never forget the day when all the expensive equipment arrived. Even with the loan, their new possessions had taken every last penny of their savings, and he and Kelly sat there without even the price of fish and chips.

Friendship and Trust

Friendship and trust were the two words that kept cropping up, over and over again, as Nick and I were discussing this present chapter. Nick and Kelly will be forever grateful to their friends in the Indi who trusted them enough to forward them a large amount of money with absolutely no collateral. Indeed subsequently Nick did not charge some Indi members for treatment at Chaucer. Not for the last time were we to recognise the importance of trust in our discussions of successful business enterprises.

During our exchanges Nick listened, disbelieving, as I introduced him to the many trendy practices that had been percolating around the business community for the past decades: Management by Objectives, Business Process Re-engineering, Enterprise Resource Planning, Balanced Score Cards, Knowledge Management etc. Just like the little boy in the crowd waving at the naked emperor strut his non-existent suit of clothes down the street, a baffled Nick would exclaim in amazement. "Why! These managers cheer on management methods just because everybody else is cheering. These methodolic businessmen and women are just like drunks, so focused on satisfying their own addiction, that they end up trusting no one, themselves included, and cynically manipulate and take advantage of anyone and everyone around them. Not surprisingly, that lack of trust is reciprocated by colleagues, which in the mind of the methodolic only goes to justify their original lack of trust."

Nick laughed when I showed him the book by Francis Fukuyama (*Trust: the Social Virtues and the Creation of Prosperity*, Simon and Schuster, New York, 1996), and explained how Trust was another popular buzzword in management circles. "And I bet they use depersonalised methods based on a lack of trust to show how to get it - but not give it. They just want to take advantage!" Nick had been there, done that. Most of his time as an untrustworthy drunk was spent spinning a web of deception (including self-deception), in order to convince those around him that he was worthy of their trust, just so that he could take advantage. "As an alcoholic I spent years perfecting arrogance, deceit, conceit, illusion, delusion and dishonesty." Expect the same from methodolics. In contrast, today's sober Nick doesn't talk about trust; he just proves he is trustworthy.

Dustmen by Day - Managing Directors by Night

Then finally in January 1978, thanks to the trust placed in them by dear friends, the fateful day arrived. Nick and Kelly were ready. They set out on a 39-week tour of the so-called 'Northern Club Circuit.' These were the Workingmen's Clubs that thrived, until the mid-eighties, in the North of England; some in Scotland, Wales, and even as far south as Slough and the outskirts of London warranted the honorary title. Often based in deprived areas, they were the nightly and often sole focal point of entertainment for an industrial or mining community.

The Northern Clubs were a law unto themselves. Nick found himself catapulted into another alien culture, just as peculiar as that of his gangster cronies from the East End, but thankfully not nearly as sinister. Having been introduced to the concept of a sub-culture when we were discussing material for the previous chapter, Nick laughingly took on the garb of an experienced anthropologist during the writing of the present chapter. He began recounting his experiences of this club-sub-culture as if he had been setting out on an expedition into the wilds of deepest Northern England. Now he sees the Club circuit as an amazing organisational culture. However that culture was not the product of a deliberate design, rather one that evolved over the years, almost by accident - just like so many companies, just like the Chaucer Clinic in fact.

As for the archetypal characters he met along his way North, their self-important egos would be recognisable to anyone who works in a major corporation. Although the men who took charge of these clubs were ordinary working class blokes holding down humble jobs during the day, they would become tyrannical senior management executives and overbearing managing directors at night. Nick had to learn how to deal with these 'little Hitlers,' but those lessons have served him well in later years. He is amazed that the skills he now depends on when running Chaucer seem to have been the result of some natural selection of accidents that popped out of his experiences from these times.

Part of managing his clinic requires him to attend the numerous interminable committee meetings that are the lifeblood of those bureaucratic organisations whose sole purpose is to regulate (or rather to interfere with) the running of health sector companies like Chaucer. Thankfully they do come across a few well-meaning, constructive and helpful administrators. However, these are more than matched by other puffed-up self-important nonentities. As we shall see later, the stupidity of these 'pensions in waiting' knows no bounds. When confronted with a particular piece of idiocy, Nick knows exactly what to do to avoid his natural but counterproductive response of getting angry; his tactic is to think of the particular idiot concerned as the President of a Northern Social Club.

The antics of these Club Presidents, Entertainment Secretaries, and their acolytes were preposterous, farcical. Nick and Kelly were introduced to the type at their very first show; they very nearly packed up and went home. Fred, the organist who was to accompany their performance, had a massive heart attack. He died just where he sat, at the organ. After the initial shock, the club members respectfully covered up the body with the organ cover. Then the audience continued happily with the serious matter of bingo: "Fred would have wanted it this way!"

An emergency Committee meeting was convened in the artist's dressing room in front of Nick and Kelly. Nick said they couldn't go on without backing. Who could play the organ to the required standard? The same shocked expression dawned on all the locals' faces; the only suitable candidate was Fred's wife. But would she perform at this time of her great loss? The six committee members turned to the wily old club President. "Fred's wife don't know 'e won't be 'ome t'night." Then looking straight at Nick he said, "so who's goin' t'ask 'er to come down t'club and play t' organ?"

Kelly whispered sarcastically to Nick, "I hope they'll have moved the body by the time you get back with Fred's wife." They learned a lot about business priorities and the single-mindedness of management on their first night on the Northern Club circuit.

At another club, the show was held up because the club President was due to address the members in the concert hall on a very important matter. The room was vast, and the audience at the back was invisible from the stage; they would disappear behind clouds of cigarette smoke. A ramp was placed leading up to the stage. The room went silent.

Everyone stood in reverence as the doors at the back crashed open, and the great man arrived. A Woodbine smouldering between his fingers, his skin a jaundiced yellow, he was clearly in the early stages of rigor mortis. Minders pushed him along in a wheelchair, up the ramp, until there he sat centre stage, microphones strategically placed on either side. Only the occasional cancerous cough broke the silence.

The great man addressed his audience: "Ladies and Gentlemen, brothers and sisters, and everyone who loves this famous club of ours. It is with deepest and sincerest regret I 'ave to inform you all, at this, our wonderful palace of entertainment, that Arthur, our much beloved entertainment secretary 'as this day received a letter from t' Abba pop group, saying they are not prepared t' play at our beloved club."

The orator was interrupted by gasps of disbelief from the audience. He paused, and nodded in sympathy before continuing. "Yes, brothers and sisters, I share your pain. But I'd like to tell you that t'Committee 'ave met, and a 'istorical decision 'as been arrived at. The Abba pop group 'ave been banned from this our beloved club, and all their records 'ave been taken off t'juke box." Resounding cheers and applause accompanied his exit. Cometh the day, cometh the CEO!

How are the Mighty Fallen

These clubs were a peculiar mix of the primitive and the ultra sophisticated. One particular club in the Northeast had a lighting system to rival anything on Broadway, but the names of each night's artistes were scribbled in chalk on a blackboard strategically placed in the foyer. On Nick and Kelly's first appearance there, the board announced: starring Solomon King, with supporting act Nick Charles and Kelly Miller. King was a big draw after his smash hit *She Wears My Ring* had reached 'the top of the hit parade' some years earlier - nostalgia was in vogue.

Suddenly the Social Secretary crashed through the front doors, hurried up to the blackboard and started rubbing out King's name, muttering profanities under his breath. It now read: starring Nick Charles and Kelly Miller, supported by Solomon King (in tiny letters).

"You can't do that," said Nick. "Solomon King is a star. He's had hit records."
"'e's no f*****g star t' me. The f*****g **** 'as just crashed into me car in t' car park."

King and all the other artistes really did need the Wisdom of Solomon to put up with the sadistic streak that regularly surfaced in the management of these clubs. The audiences too would take a perverse pride in "bringing mister 'igh and mighty down a peg or two." One club in the Midlands went as far as placing a brass plate on the wall of the artistes' dressing room that proudly trumpeted: "Englebert Humperdinck once died a death here." A club in Grimsby used to pay acts an extra £50 each for Sunday performances. The audience would enter stocked up with rotten tomatoes just to throw at the performers, no matter how well they performed. None of Nick and Kelly's hard-earned posh stage-clothes was worn at that venue!

The Laburnum Mystery
On another occasion Nick and Kelly arrived at the Laburnum Trades and Labour Club to find it surrounded by police cars, blue lights flashing. Policemen covered the place like a rash. Confused, Nick entered the reception area. "We're the cabaret," he said to the man sporting a badge labelling him the Entertainment Secretary.

"Sorry about this, but we've had a mysterious break-in." The club's complicated alarm system had been breached. To enter, the thieves first had to bypass the alarms on all doors and windows. Then they had to get through an alarmed metal cage securing the bar and tills.

Looking towards the other side of the room, past a draped monolith at the edge of the stage, Nick could see a very irritated Bar Manager raising his voice to his police inquisitor: "Superintendent, just 'ow many times do I 'ave t' tell you? We've 'ad a break-in, but nowt's bin stolen!"

"Do you mean to tell me that someone managed to breach two of the most sophisticated alarm systems in Yorkshire, and then they just left, not nicking nothing? Not so much as a nip of whisky?"

"I'll tell you one more time. I arrived at 2.30pm, the same time as always." The Manager went through the afternoon's events right up to the police arriving. "And I've checked over and over again … there's nowt missing!"

Meanwhile Nick and Kelly were being ushered away from the reception area by the entertainment secretary, and shown into the artistes' dressing rooms. They were now old hands on the club circuit and so were used to being told how this or that particular club had the best backing band in the whole country. "And what's more, our organ cost a king's ransom, the like of which you've never seen before." He proudly pointed at the rectangular block draped in a dustsheet that Nick had spotted earlier. "The backing should be good tonight." Nick murmured appreciatively, and Kelly nodded her agreement.

In the distance the tone suddenly changed. An assistant barman had approached the Bar Manager. There were raised voices. "Wad'yer mean there's 36 empty wooden crates missing?"

The policeman was shaking his head in total disbelief: "They bypass two of the most sophisticated alarms known to man, and you're telling me that all they've nicked is 36 bloody empty beer crates?" The poor assistant nodded nervously, shifting from one foot to the other, but he said nothing more.

Nick and Kelly were finally given permission to unload their equipment and set up for the forthcoming show. Eventually the police melted away and the club slowly began to take on its normal ambience. Two hours later Nick and Kelly, elegantly dressed in their sequinned stage clothes, duly awaited the arrival of the musicians for the customary band-call. When they arrived, they too extolled the virtues of the club organ, which "had cost £100,000 and was the best money could buy." Dutifully, the drummer, guitarist and bass player stood at the appropriate corners and, with a flourish, whisked off the dust covers, to reveal … 36 wooden beer crates neatly stacked in the shape of the organ's silhouette.

A Miner Detail

Nick and Kelly's first booking at a miner's club in Castleford, Yorkshire was an experience they will never forget. It was a Sunday morning and they walked onto the stage to face an audience composed of ... hundreds of copies of the *News of the World*. The only movement they could discern was the occasional turning of a page, or a pint of beer being downed.

"We'll soon shake this lot up," said Nick. They were scheduled to perform two thirty-minute spots. The first number came to an immaculate close, ably backed by a super six-piece band. "Thank you, thank you," said Nick to the audience in his customary fashion, a sentiment enthusiastically echoed by Kelly. But there was no applause, just silence punctuated by the odd smoker's cough. The only visible reaction appeared to be a few hundred grimy thumbs sticking up from behind the Sunday newspapers, the odd forefinger implying something should be stuffed where the monkey puts his nuts, and a few two fingered messages. Nick couldn't decide whether they were V for victory, or go forth and multiply!

The entire first 30 minutes, although immaculately presented, finished in the same deafening silence, and the odd ruffle of newspaper pages. Nick and Kelly knew they had put on a great performance, and yet they left the stage to the hollow sound of their own footsteps. As they descended from the wings down a small stairway an enthusiastic entertainment secretary, beaming from ear to ear, met them.
"Ah! Lad, yoo've got a greet act theer," he enthused.
"You must be joking," said Nick. "We've just done 30 minutes, and we didn't receive a single clap."
Just then a black-faced miner walked by, covered from head to foot in coal dust and sporting a traditional safety helmet, complete with lamp. Before the entertainment secretary could reply, the miner chipped in: "They daun't clap us, lad, when we come up outta pit!"

He could live for a thousand years, Nick thought, and still not truly understand the alien culture North of Watford. Here were English people, who were living a mere couple of hundred miles from London, but they may as well have come from another planet.

End of the World

Stories! Nick's got thousand's of 'em. He has so many happy memories of their successes on the circuit, and no memory is happier than their choice of keyboard player when he and Kelly decided to extend their duo into a trio. Teresa Weiler, the second of the three most important women in Nick's life, appeared on the scene at the end of 1980, and moved into their house with them. Teresa would accompany them to clubs that could not supply their own backing group. When she was not on tour with Nick and Kelly, she stayed in the house in Hounslow.

In total she only did about thirty performances, but it wasn't long before Nick spotted her natural talent for bringing order to the chaos of his business affairs. Teresa soon became indispensable, as we will see in the following chapters. Twenty-five years on and she is still with them, although now as the Business Manager of Chaucer, advisor to the Managing Director, Secretary to three limited companies, and PA/Secretary to the Trustees of the Charitable Foundation.

The lessons Nick learned in dealing with the management of Northern Clubs, a group of people whose way of life, and sets of priorities, were (and perhaps still are) so incomprehensible to him, convinced Nick that from then on he should never be blasé when coming into contact with the group dynamics of such an alien culture. "There's nowt so queer as folk." This personal understanding has served him well, when, for example, he has had to confront the perversity of some health-service bureaucrats inhabiting a poisonous sub-culture that makes the sadism of the Northern Clubs seem positively benign.

However, all good things eventually come to an end. Even in their death throes in the mid-eighties, the Northern Clubs left Nick a legacy of one final and very valuable lesson. Don't get too complacent. When things are going too well, when something is too good to be true, then it isn't … either good or true. Someone is sure to come along, usually a politician, and wreck it. So it was that Prime Minister Margaret Thatcher decided to have a showdown with the National Miners' Union and its troublesome leader, Arthur Scargill. A year-long miners' strike, starting in 1984, caused a haemorrhage of the wealth in the area, and finally drove many of the clubs, already teetering on the edge, to fall over into bankruptcy. Ten thousand club acts disappeared into obscurity, it seemed like almost overnight, and a way of life disappeared forever.

The bookings on the circuit were drying up. On February 17, 1985 Nick and Kelly were asked to stand in at short notice at the Faraday Ex-servicemen's Club in Slough. As they walked off stage that night, applause ringing in their ears, after more than sixteen hundred performances and more than seven years on the circuit, little did they realise that Nick Charles and Kelly Miller would never again appear on a club stage.

But as Nick, ever the optimist says: 'As one door closes, another opens!' And with the support of Teresa beavering away down in Hounslow, for quite some time Nick the entrepreneur had been opening many other doors as sidelines. Now those sidelines would have to become his main source of income.

6

Entrepreneurship - "I can do that"

Nick the entrepreneur is never far from the surface of his personality. Even the scams he pulled when he was an alcoholic were in essence a muddled form of entrepreneurship, and not, as could be supposed, just the deviousness of a drunk.

Scotch Cognac?

Like the time that Nick was appearing at a Bournemouth hotel, and was under threat of a fate worse than death if he failed to make his next booking the following day in Scotland. It was a very long journey, but the money was too good to miss. To ensure his compliance Vanessa Heath, his 'manager,' insisted that she accompany him on what was to be an alcohol-free journey.

Or so she thought! While Vanessa slept snugly in her hotel bed, Nick crept downstairs to rig up a tube that ran from the windscreen-washer bottle to emerge alongside the steering column.

Having filled the washer bottle with brandy, all Nick had to do on the journey was lean forward and suck the booze, while his companion travelled oblivious of the gadget. There was only one flaw with the plan: no matter how hard he sucked the golden liquid refused to travel along the tube.

Just to prove that his education wasn't wasted, Nick realised this was due to unequal air pressure between the inside and outside of the bottle. He was a drunk, but he wasn't stupid. So with the help of the friendly night porter, another alcoholic, he went into the hotel kitchen and heated a meat skewer until it was red hot. Holding it gingerly with a kitchen mitt, Nick skewered a hole in the polythene lid of the washer bottle, thereby balancing the air pressure. He didn't stop for a single drink on his journey to Scotland. "Such a good boy!"

More by Luck?

Once he was out of the clutches of the demon drink and performing on the Northern Club circuit, these innovative skills were given a free and far more constructive rein. Nick has always been a dynamo, his only problem was, and still is, how to focus that enormous energy. Naturally he would spend much of his time while on the circuit rehearsing or performing his cabaret act with Kelly. However, he is also driven by his own personal demons to make time to help the many drunks who come to him with their problems (see the next chapter). He has never forgotten his promise to Harry's Hat on the steps below London Bridge. Within six months of drying himself out he was operating day centres to help these unfortunates.

Not satisfied with his workload, he would also come up with innumerable entrepreneurial schemes, possibly far too many, to help pay for running the centres. Nick needed a steadying hand, not only to put a brake on the more extreme excesses of his imagination, but also to ensure that his viable ideas were sensibly implemented, and followed through; he couldn't afford too many exploding Guinness bottles! That someone also needed to guarantee that his ideas, when implemented, were pursued within sensible financial and economic constraints. More by luck than judgement, Nick already had such a levelheaded paragon living with him and Kelly in their house in Hounslow: Teresa Weiler.

'More by luck than judgement?' I have found myself saying these words far too many times when describing Nick's business ventures. Perhaps luck has nothing to do with it? Perhaps Nick makes his own luck? I recalled something Nick said to me in one of our very first meetings: "We all live in exactly the same world, only I'm more aware of the extremes - and they are more aware of me." Perhaps, by opening himself up to these extremes, by embracing uncertainty, Nick makes his own luck in the natural selection of accidents that is the way he runs his business and his life?

Before embarking on writing this present chapter, I asked Nick the entrepreneur what he meant by the term 'entrepreneur.' Nick, being Nick, started by talking about what it wasn't.

"My kind of entrepreneurship has nothing to do with inventing things, in the sense of a long period of research and development that culminates in a product. Entrepreneurship, to me, is about contacts and connections. It is all to do with making a spontaneous connection between previous experiences and relationships, out of which pop opportunities; it is about having the 'knack' to see such opportunities and then following it through. Everyone has the ability to see such opportunities, but the prospects must be exploited or they will just dissipate. Most people are cowards; they are risk-averse, inert, and they take the easy route by denying that chances even appear to them."

Nick's approach is best summed up in one of his favourite sentences: "I can do that." Shoot first and ask questions later. But he realises that he can't do it all on his own, because although his unbridled enthusiasm will throw up a million and one connections, he knows most of them are ridiculous, many of them dubious. "There are opportunities everywhere. We're falling all over them. All we have to do is look - or rather see. My talent, and my problem, is that I see too many opportunities, and I can't differentiate between the sublime and the ridiculous." He needed (and still needs) level heads around him, to tell him when to start, when to see his ideas through, but most importantly when to stop. "An effective entrepreneur knows when he needs help, and rejects the poor advice but acts on the good."

Beer and Skittles; Contacts and Connections

At the core of Nick's approach to making innovative connections is his enormous network of contacts - he prefers to call them friends - assiduously nurtured over the years. This was certainly the case with his first major venture into showbiz management when, over a very short period of time, he put together a highly effective entertainment programme for the Watney's 'Managed House' brewery chain: again contacts and connections.

Nick and Kelly had made many good contacts when they were performing on the Northern Club circuit, and they shared their friends' financial problems with its collapse. But every cloud has a silver lining. Nick connected the dire prospects they all faced to his (second-to-none) knowledge of the London pub scene. His brainwave was bringing the acts to perform in public houses in and around London, where previously there had been no equivalent quality to the Northern club scene.

"I can do that." There were problems of course. It's one thing seeing the big picture, quite another dealing with the devil in the details. Nick had routed that devil many times before, and he is confident that he has the skills to see off all future diabolical problems. His first problem with the Watney's scheme was the fact that no single pub could afford the £600 per week that a Northern act would typically charge. Nick wasn't put off.

From personal experience he knew that acts would have to find food, board, travel expenses and all the other costs out of that money; and they had to factor in the nights off in the week when there was no work. Nick figured that he would create a co-operative. The entertainers would lodge in the pubs and eat bar food for free. Since there was a minimum of travel (cars were only needed to carry equipment short distances), and less expensive costumes, by paying the entertainers £200 per week, they would in fact be better off.

He first convinced some of his closer contacts from the club circuit of the merits of his scheme; but he still had to make it work. Or rather he did what Nick does best: he left it to Teresa to make it work. She calculated that if the acts worked six nights per week, then six acts could cover a circuit of 18 pubs, each doing 6 shows per week. Within no time they had ten circuits, each of 18 pubs. At one point it even rose to 25 circuits, 450 pubs in total.

The money started rolling in, but there was still only the three of them running it all. As agents for the acts, Nick, Kelly and Teresa would frantically run around London taking bookings and picking up moneys owed. It was exhilarating, but exhausting. On one occasion they staggered home to Hounslow in the early hours so tired that they left £15,000 in cash on the back seat of their car, which stood unlocked outside their house. Luckily Kelly, waking up around dawn to let out the cat, remembered the money and rushed out to retrieve it.

Bolstered by their success they began re-investing their profits in their business. Things were going well ... too well. Without warning, the man from Watney's, the Leisure Services Director who had backed their initiative, committed suicide. His replacement did what every new appointee who is uncertain of his new position would do: he played the 'new broom' gambit to demonstrate that he was in control of events. Everything his predecessor had supported had to go. He scrapped the contract with Nick, claiming that the acts weren't bringing in enough money to justify the expense. Customers, he said, were watching the acts and not buying drinks. It was back to square one with very little to show for the rollercoaster ride.

The Fight Game

While they were juggling their pub circuits, Nick was still running the day centres for alcoholics. One of those he was helping was John Conteh, the ex-World Light Heavyweight boxing champion. Nick would visit John's home selling sobriety perhaps two or three times each week for a whole year. He would manage to keep John off the sauce for a few weeks, but then without warning John would go off on another bender.

The whole destructive sequence would be repeated over and over and over again. On one occasion he found John climbing the kitchen floor. Nick totally lost his rag. Screaming and shouting, he jumped on top of John, grabbing his head and shaking him violently. Nick suddenly stopped and starting laughing, realising what he was doing: he had grabbed the light heavyweight champion of the world by the throat, and lived to tell the tale! It was just as well that John was totally incapacitated by drink. All's well that ends well! Nick was eventually successful in leading John to sobriety. Conteh went on to lead an exemplary life.

While Nick was spending all this time with John Conteh, he was mixing with John's handlers and others in the wider boxing community. Everyone who met Nick realised immediately that he has a flair for selling and for publicity. Hence it was no surprise that boxing impresario Bobby Naidoo asked Nick if he wanted the contract to sell advertising space on the corners and ringside billboards for a couple of his major title fights. "I can do that." This is how Nick the entrepreneur works. His contacts ask him if he is interested in a particular contract selling or promoting whatever.

He then connects with other contacts, does a huge amount of homework so that he knows all about the job at hand, and then delivers a great job. His networks remember this, and the virtuous circle is reinforced. Then, whenever a new job crops up, his name is always one of the first to be thrown in the ring.

It is still happening today, although because he has his hands full with Chaucer, he regretfully passes them on to others that he thinks might be able to help. However, even today, if money is tight, Nick dusts off his old entrepreneurial skills to help fund the Clinic. Back then it was different; money was always tight and so he was always on the lookout for new opportunities. Nick thought he had found the 'big one' when he accompanied John Conteh to a boxing match in the Midlands. There he saw an excellent up-and-coming young boxer in one of the minor bouts. The boxer's trainer was looking for an investor, and someone to manage the 'contender.'

"I can do that," said Nick and he set out organising things. All was going well until, at another bout just a few weeks later, a sinister stranger whose hands were firmly jammed into the pockets of his dark trench coat approached Nick. It was just like in the movies. The man slowly raised his right hand to waist height, but still keeping it in his pocket. "I've got a gun. If you know what's good for you, you'll forget about being a fight manager." Nick did know what was good for him, and that included not dealing with people like this. So he just walked away from the fight game, and didn't look back. "The real trick in entrepreneurship is not only knowing when to act, but also when to walk away."

He didn't need that sort of aggravation, particularly since he had many more irons in the fire. Always on the lookout for business opportunities, Nick had helped organise sponsorship for Eve Jackson, the young woman who completed the amazing feat of flying around the globe in a micro-light aircraft. He was also considering managing an extremely talented actress Sian Howard, and he even hatched a complicated plot to have her play the part of Eve in the film of the book of the epic journey. He would have a piece of the book, the film and the actress: an agent's heaven. Unfortunately that deal fell through, although he did set up another book deal for a lady who had sledged around the Arctic only to crash into a polar bear!

Naked Ambition

With all these deals percolating around the business community Nick was getting better known among the other agents and their clients, and he always had a reputation of being straight. Unfortunately his clients didn't always reciprocate. One ran off with sufficient funds to buy a Ferrari, only to write it off, uninsured, just a few hundred yards from the Maranello showroom. With his links in the newspaper and magazine world developed while in the fight game, and his contacts in the more seedier side of boxing, he was being approached by what today are euphemistically called 'glamour models' - the topless (and more) posers who adorn Page Three of the 'red tops' - to get their photographs in the magazines and newspapers.

"I can do that." Word of mouth recommendations soon brought him a string of 'models' and striptease artistes, and it wasn't long before Nick decided to move his business along the supply chain. He discovered that Teresa, who by now was a permanent member of Nick Charles Enterprises, had another commercially viable talent: she was an excellent photographer. All the angles were covered: Kelly would help the girls with their make up and clothing (what little there was of it), Teresa would take the photographs, and Nick would market and sell them to the newspapers and magazines. Together they would also develop and print the photos. It was quite a conveyor belt. They roped in one of Nick's clients, a 'risqué' comedian named Geoff Single a.k.a. Martin Jackson. All four would stand in a production line in Geoff's blacked-out bedroom in his mother's council flat in Bethnal Green. There was Teresa at one end developing the negatives, Nick and Geoff projecting and printing, with Kelly drying and pegging the prints on a line.

Some days they had so many orders for photographs that they had no time to eat. Because their hands were covered in chemicals, Geoff's mum would come in and feed sandwiches directly into their mouths, so that all four could keep up the non-stop processing. During this feeding frenzy mum would sometimes look down at the photographs, all the while tut-tut-ing, now and then exclaiming "disgusting" or "am they real!" at particularly notable images. She obviously had no idea what her darling son did for a living! (See **Drawing the Line** below).

Nick's girls didn't just appear in the newspapers. For a short period during the early eighties some of the colour magazines had started printing a few monochrome 'glamour shots' among their colour spreads. Nick had convinced them of the 'artistic merit' of black and white photos over colour. That wasn't his real reason of course. His production line could only print in black and white; all the colour processing had to be sent out to expensive third parties, cutting into his profits.

Seeing where their photographs were being published it was only a matter of time before Nick decided: "I can do that." So he opened his own magazine, naturally enough entitled *Page Three Magazine*. Nick was amazed to find that the Sun newspaper, which started the whole Page Three phenomenon, didn't own rights to the name at the time. The team would cut and paste the text for the magazine, and print out the copy, minus photographs, using a photocopier. The photos were then glued on top, and then the whole magazine was taken to a commercial printer. The magazines were aimed at around four hundred 'adult' venues, and ran to four editions before Nick sold out his share to his sleeping partner. Teresa, business-minded as ever, and always one for the legalities of the situation, discovered that they needed to be licensed to produce these magazines. Obtaining the necessary licences would take too much time, effort, and money, so again they sold up, and just walked away.

Drawing the Line

Nick wasn't just an agent for models; Geoff, from the photographic production line, was also on his books as an 'adult comedian' and master of ceremonies at stag nights and hen parties. Nick would stake out adverts for his company's services on motorway embankments. The promise "If you want a really hot stag night or hen party call Humphrey Humbleton on 01...." would scream down on passing motorists. The Ministry of Transport was not amused. Advertising on motorways is illegal, and they phoned the number 01... so generously supplied by Nick on his hoardings, and told him in no uncertain terms to stop.

Nick draws the line at breaking the law, so he immediately took down his large placards ... and replaced them with bigger new ones, now stating "This is NOT an advertisement. If you want a really hot stag night or hen party DON'T call Humphrey

Humbleton on 01...." Nick heard no more from the Ministry, although he did notice that he had to replace the non-adverts at more frequent intervals as the originals tended to disappear.

There were two types of show on offer: a £400 show or an £800 show. Teresa would take the telephone bookings and collect the money. When she asked Geoff about the difference between the two shows, so that she could explain to potential customers, she was told: "The £400 stops short of the line; the £800 goes over the line." She passed this quotation on to whoever inquired, having not the slightest idea what Geoff meant, and thought no more about it. Teresa simply told herself that the more expensive show was merely longer with more acts. Then on one of the nights when Teresa was out and about collecting payments, she arrived early at a £800 show in Richmond only to see live sex on stage: "Over the line" meant "all the way." Having had no idea that Geoff had been using their agency for what was probably illegal, she quietly but hurriedly removed the £800 shows from their books.

But things were going downhill in the glamour business. Whatever its promoters say, it had nothing to do with alternative life-styles. It was, and still is, a shady and distasteful business. Nick Charles Enterprises treated the girls decently, which is why they sought him out as an agent. However, the girls themselves were getting to be far too much trouble. Here was Nick running centres for drunks during the day, and yet at night he was involved in a sordid business that was driving many of the girls, voluntarily it must be said, towards alcohol and drugs. It all came to a head in Raymond's Revue Bar in London's Soho. Nick and Teresa had booked a girl into the 'erotic cabaret,' and were there checking up on the act. Teresa looked at Nick and said: "my dad didn't bring me up to do this." Nick nodded, and yet again without regrets they got up and walked out of the show and away from the whole business, never looking back.

Theatrical Behaviour

He didn't have to worry because with all the experience and exposure he was getting, Nick's telephone would ring with fresh offers every day. Soon after leaving the questionable world of 'glamour,' the phone rang and a very posh voice said, "I hear you're a damn fine publicist. Need one. Have a play - *Daisy Pulls It Off* - you know. Going on tour. Are you game? What?"

"I can do that," came out immediately. The deal was done, and the fees agreed in just a few minutes. Replacing the phone, Nick turned to Teresa and asked, "what's a publicist?"

To which Teresa, as sharp as ever, replied: "It's what you do all the time, only its where you publicise something other than yourself." Nothing succeeds like success. The word soon got around, and within days he was also publicising the repertory tour of *No Sex Please We're British*. *Home Is Where Your Clothes Are* followed, and then two pantomimes *Cinderella* and *Snow White*. These were all nice little earners, but unfortunately they all ended at roughly the same time.

Nothing fails like success. The phones suddenly stopped ringing. It turned out that the audiences in British provincial theatres were in serious decline, and rather than pay for the publicity, touring companies had started to use the theatres' own PR machinery. Nick was never one to hold out false hopes. He knows there is no fighting back when the fundamental economic realities of a business sector have changed forever. In this situation the sensible tactic is to cut and run.

There was, however, one final telephone call. A famous theatrical producer wanted to know if Nick would publicise a production starring Charlton Heston. "I can do that." "I've just got a licence for an alcoholics clinic, and at the moment I've got a graphic artist and two journalists among my patients looking for work therapy. We can put the project together in two ticks." At the mere mention of the word alcoholic the phone went dead. Nick was about to discover that denial is a very powerful force. He should have realised that talk of alcoholism is not welcome anywhere! Most people would rather not know: 'Out of sight, out of mind.' The word of Nick's involvement with alcoholics spread like wildfire, and that was the end of Nick the theatrical publicist. The networks that build you up, if you offend their sensibilities, even accidentally, even with good intentions, can bring you down in an instant.

The Birth of Chaucer

While all this was going on, the day centres were going from strength to strength, although the money was getting tighter with the diminishing cross-subsidies from his other enterprises. With less external distractions Nick threw himself even more energetically into helping the drunks. Kelly was just as active, with the job of driving around the 'manor' picking up patients, ferrying them to medical appointments, and delivering publicity material and other information around local hospitals and doctors' surgeries.

At one point the money disappeared altogether. Teresa went to work at Carline, the car rental company, just so they would have enough money to buy food for themselves and the day centres. Then came the magic day in 1989 when a fairy godmother from the Department of Health and Social Security, based in Glasgow, telephoned. They wished to transfer three patients to the day centre, which by now had been named Chaucer. For once the answer wasn't "I can do that," mainly because by chance Teresa had popped in from her job at Carline, and it was she who answered the phone. She replied: "But we are a day-clinic, not residential."

The very insistent Scottish lady wouldn't be put off, and continued, quite reasonably: "So why can't they sleep in the clinic."
"We don't have a licence."
"I can give you licence for three people over the phone if your clinic fits the right criteria: would they have a bed? A bedside lamp? And toilets?"
"Yes, to all those requirements, and they also have showers."
"What about food?"
"We have kitchens in which we cook them breakfast, lunch and tea."
"Done. They are on their way to you. That's £750 per week for the three people. I suggest you start the formal paperwork for accepting more patients."
"I can do that." Nick's catch phrase was ... catching. In that moment, what had started out as Nick's privately funded charity to help fellow drunks had now become a self-funding not-for-profit organisation.

However, that was not in the mind of the accountant who came to check the books of the Clinic as part of the formal licensing procedure. What he found was Nick's accounting system of two buckets, one containing money, and the other bills. It was time to bring Teresa in to manage the Clinic full time. Nick promised her the earth - quite a promise on the back of Chaucer's income of

£750 per week. Teresa left Carline, and took on the job of business manager for Chaucer. Of course Nick's projections, like all entrepreneurs, were over-optimistic, and it was quite a few years before he could fulfil his promises to her. "Yes I did promise you a good salary, a car and house, but I didn't say in which year you'd get them." Teresa knew Nick well enough to realise that he would eventually deliver. Sure enough some years later she did get the salary, car and house he had promised. To this day she still fills her working hours and beyond, shining the cold light of reason on Nick's more excessive schemes.

7

The Nick Charles Day Centres

From the moment he gave up drinking on that fateful December morning in 1976, Nick knew that he would help fellow seekers after sobriety. This was only to be expected: all newly sober drunks profess the same proselytising urge. They talk about it a lot; it can be a crutch to help them stay sober during their early days on the wagon. What made Nick different was that he meant it. He really did intend to fulfil his vow to Harry's Hat as it floated accusingly down the Thames. His urge to help is undiminished nearly thirty years on.

Nick never does anything by half. He threw himself wholeheartedly into helping drunks, and very soon all the dossers in West-London who wanted to dry out would seek his advice. In fact, a major reason for his acceptance into the Indi (the self-help group that funded his car, house and equipment) was because of the support he gave the Southall Indian community in coping with their own alcohol abusers, a situation that just does not occur to the same scale back on the sub-continent. A leading member of the West-London Sikh community once brought a fellow Sikh to Nick. He was totally mystified because his friend managed to stay drunk despite being deprived of alcohol for several hours. Without batting an eyelid Nick pointed at his rather tall turban. Sure enough they found a plaster cast holding the headpiece in shape and hiding a quarter bottle of absinthe. It takes a drunk to know a drunk's tricks.

Waste Products
Six months into his sobriety Nick's reputation for helping alcoholics was spreading. One of the dossers told him of an abandoned public lavatory in deepest Middlesex, derelict and

covered in graffiti. Formerly run by the local council, it had recently been bought by an estate agent who hadn't the slightest idea of what to do with it. All the fittings and fixtures were ingrained with the foulest odours that had accumulated over the decades when it was a conduit for every type of human waste product.

Nick simply went up to the agent's office and asked if he could use it, rent free, as a meeting place for alcoholics. Don't believe all the bad press you hear about estate agents. This one had a great sense of humour, and generously agreed to Nick's proposal. There were conditions: that Nick's drunks would gut the building and refit it, and that they would vacate the premises whenever the agent received a profitable offer for it. The project became Nick's first work therapy/counselling day centre, open free of charge for 10 hours a day, 5 days a week. Crown Paint donated damaged cans of paint for redecoration, and the local Marks and Spencer let them have food at knockdown prices. The centre stayed open for 13 months, after which time the stench had become a distant memory and the estate agent finally managed to sell the ex-lavatory as an office.

Bureaucracy
However, Nick would soon find that the benefit of each act of generosity could be counterbalanced by some mean-spirited obstruction elsewhere. It was here in Middlesex that Nick got his first real taste of bureaucracy, a bitter taste that recurs right up to the present. He approached the Council for a grant to run his day centre, and was delighted to be invited to their offices in order to discuss funding. Ten meetings later, he naively inquired: "What sum of money can I reasonably expect?" He was told £50! "Ten meetings for £50! It must have cost the Council over a £1000 in salaries and expenses just to 'give' away that £50. It's cheaper just to throw bank notes from the top of the building." Nick, never one to suffer fools gladly, stormed out.

He was horrified that nobody, absolutely nobody, thought this situation was odd in any way. Nick suddenly appreciated the anaesthetic effect of the booze on him. Now sober, it was as though he had re-awoken after fourteen years, and he still had the social skills of a teenager, with a teenager's grudging acceptance of the power of those in authority - but with an adolescent's seething resentment of injustice and stupidity. He had thought of the local council as something significant and austere, full of important but boring old people who were engrossed in working for the good of the community. An infuriated Nick grew up in that tenth meeting. He saw a bureaucracy stacked full of jobsworths (the word is derived from 'it's more than my job's worth' ... an excuse for acting according to a mindless book of rules, rather than making a sensible decision), operating according to a logic that was no less crazy than that of the alcoholics he was trying to cure. He was to see this nonsense over and over again during the next two decades, and even after all this time he still hasn't lost his anger over all the waste and inefficiency.

However, irritation doesn't pay the bills. In the early days Nick and Kelly underwrote the operation with their earnings from the club circuit. This was before Teresa had appeared on the scene, and so while they were away on tour the day centre was left in the charge of a Team Leader, a trustee chosen from among the 'members.' During one absence the trustee had a brainwave to help raise funds. Woodworking was a major part of work therapy at the centre, so he decided that the group should make twenty wooden collection boxes. Members would go out into the community to collect funds. What returned were twenty very empty boxes carried by twenty extremely drunk collectors who had done the rounds of the local pubs.

Nick chose the term 'member' to describe those attending his day centres, as this word has more positive connotations than 'patient,' or 'client,' or worse 'inmate.' He says that alcoholics may be damaged, but they are not necessarily sick when they stop drinking; and he adds "they paid a very high membership fee for joining their club. It cost them everything they ever owned or held dear."

The Day Centre continued

After a little over a year the day finally arrived when the estate agent came to reclaim his office. Nick, about to lose his public lavatory day centre, went searching for a replacement. Again he found generous support, this time from his local GP who could see the real value in what Nick was doing. He was offered a spare room for meetings, with facilities for work therapy. Eventually Nick would move on to yet another general practice in the vicinity, where he remained for a further two years until finally having to move their operations back to their home in Hounslow. Teresa was living with them by then, and she started running the business side of operations. The day centres first operated as a non-registered charity, but as the scale of the work they had set themselves became all too clear, Nick decided to apply for full charity registration, and this was granted in December 1986.

It wasn't long before Nick became well known, far beyond just the society of dossers; he's always had a knack for raising his public profile. Soon the newspapers were contacting him whenever a story about some celebrity falling off the wagon appeared on their radar screen. Within a year of his sobriety, newspaper stories had been written about Nick and he had appeared on an ATV documentary about the Salvation Army's work with drunks: *For God's Sake Care*. Proof of the anaesthetic properties of alcohol is also apparent here; Nick has absolutely no recollection of this programme. It was only when researching data for this book that I found a TV Times article about his appearance.

Snap Happy

Around this time he received a telephone call at the day centre from a Japanese businessman, whom Nick can only assume had seen the TV programme, asking to book an appointment. The man didn't inquire into Nick's background, and Nick didn't volunteer any information. A meeting was arranged for one lunch-time in the Excelsior Hotel - quite convenient for Nick, since he spent a great deal of his time in their car park while holding down his job with NCP.

Nick changed out of his luminous yellow jacket in a hotel washroom, and at one o'clock walked smiling into the lounge. It turned out that the businessman was at his wit's end over his critically ill fifteen year-old daughter Mitsuko. She was both alcoholic and anorexic. Nick agreed that he would meet her and do his best to help. The Japanese father wanted the sessions to be once a week, but Nick said there should be at least twice-weekly sessions if there was to be any progress. The father wasn't sure, and with great difficulty, he agreed, although Nick couldn't quite see what all the fuss was about. Nick met the young lady on this basis, and over a period of weeks rapid progress was made. It was only after they got to know each other better that he understood her father's reticence. Nick was stunned to find out that the young lady was making two return flights each week from Tokyo to attend the sessions; he had thought that she was based in London. However, all's well that ends well. Mitsuko is now nearing forty years-of-age, married with children of her own, eats normally, and has not had an alcoholic drink since.

Finding any time at all to help this young lady had been a logistical nightmare. She thought that Nick was a successful professional entertainer who spent his spare time treating alcoholics. Consequently he was reluctant to admit to treating alcoholics part-time, all the while working twelve-hour shifts, seven days a week for National Car Parks. He spent his time driving passengers between the airport and the Excelsior Car Park. By coincidence Mitsuko would stay at the Excelsior during her stay in England, and so over the weeks Nick had a few tricky moments avoiding being spotted. One day towards the end of her treatment, almost inevitably, she spotted Nick glowing bright yellow in his NCP jacket. Waving Nick over, she asked if she could be photographed with him, as a memento. Innocently she inquired what the letters NCP stood for. In a flash Nick told her: Nick Charles Personnel. She had her photo taken, but only after Nick had removed the incriminating garment.

Runaway

At no point did Nick talk about payment, and he was very pleasantly surprised when, some time later, a substantial cheque appeared from a very grateful father. Nick also helped the young actress daughter of an American film dynasty, who had been introduced by Del Shannon the American pop singer. The dynasty also expressed its gratitude with a cheque. Maybe, just maybe, Nick thought, it was possible to raise the funding that would put his day centres on a proper financial footing. Never in his wildest dreams did he foresee Chaucer; but that was still ten years away.

Nick had first met Del Shannon in 1962, during his tour of Britain that followed the hit song *Runaway*. A sixteen-year-old Nick was in a supporting band at the Walthamstow Granada. It was 1979 before they met again; Del was playing at a venue across the road from the club where Nick and Kelly were in cabaret. Nick sent a note backstage to Del asking if he remembered Freddy 'Boom Boom' Cannon smashing up a piano at Walthamstow. He did.

They were invited backstage, and to cut a long story short, Del ended up by staying for a while at Nick and Kelly's home in Hounslow, before returning to the USA.

As fate would have it, Del too had a serious drink problem. "I've got a disease called I ain't got it," is how he graphically described his situation. Nick tried to help, but Del returned to the USA where the problem worsened. Then out of the blue Del decided to jump on a plane back to England to complete Nick's programme. When Del returned home to America, Nick would write him letters to keep him on the straight and narrow; but Del had other serious problems. A manic-depressive, he did manage to stay sober for twelve years, before tragically committing suicide soon after starting a new course of tablets aimed at helping his depression. "These new pills are making my brain fizz," were his words to Kelly in one of the very last telephone calls he ever made.

It was also in 1979 that Nick made another of those special contacts, a friendship that would change his life forever. This time it was Dr. David Marjot, Regional Addiction Consultant based at St. Bernard's Hospital, who had the foresight to see the value of what Nick was trying to do for the drunks in his area. Nick had sufficient facilities in his day centres for a so-called 'community detox.' He could help those members who did not require medical supervision during detoxification. Those extreme cases needing a 'residential detox' had to be referred to a hospital ward under medical supervision. Here was true synergy. Nick would send those members needing residential treatment to Dr. Marjot, and he would send to Nick those patients in his care who could be treated in the community.

Everybody gained. Nick had the support of a highly respected member of the medical profession; Dr. Marjot could use his own scarce resources far more efficiently. In 2005 progress (!) in the guise of the Primary Care Trust would see the end of this scheme, deeming it perilous.

One Minute Fifty Seconds that Changed Nick's Life

Whenever Nick came across anyone with a booze problem he would do his utmost to help. This was the case with Jimmy Greaves, the well-known professional footballer, who was famously left out of the English football team that won the 1966

World Cup. Even before that very public humiliation, Jimmy drank to excess, but subsequently he spiralled downward, completely out of control. He would complete detox programmes, only to set off on benders immediately on checking out. Of course, someone that famous couldn't keep his addiction secret for long. It was inevitable that the press would be tipped off on one of the occasions he booked into the psychiatric ward of Warley Hospital. Sure enough, Frank Thorne of the *Sunday People* got hold of the story, and on February 12th 1978 the headline 'Drink is Killing Me,' says Jimmy Greaves was splashed all over the front page.

Having previously tried and failed to kick the habit, the shame of this notoriety finally gave Greaves the strength to escape the clutches of alcoholism. "That article hurt so badly, I really made a final effort to pull myself together." He received hundreds of letters of support following that article, and one in particular from Nick "really hit home." "Just reading his letter once was enough to sober me up."

Jimmy still keeps that letter, which finished with Nick saying: "If I can do it mate, so can you." True to form, Jimmy himself set out to share his experiences in order to help other alcoholics. When Jimmy's autobiography *This One's on Me* was published it was inevitable that the media would be interested in his story. Sure enough a television programme *Just for Today* was produced for ATV, and broadcast across on the ITV network in 1980.

Jimmy had told the producers about Nick and his letter, and so Nick and Kelly were invited on to the programme. It was a small slot. Nick appeared on screen for a mere one minute and fifty seconds, but they were to change his life. For it was in those few moments that Nick unwittingly took the first tentative steps towards Chaucer. Looking straight at camera, he said, "Alcoholism is cancer of the soul." That short sentence resonated around the television audience, and soon the letters began to pour in.

Nick and Kelly were touring the clubs at this time, and it was very common for him to be introduced as "the famous drunk from London who appeared on the Jimmy Greaves story." After every performance of the act with Kelly, people worried about family members with drink problems would approach them.

The Last Day Centre

While they were on the road, Teresa in Hounslow would be handling the mail and the telephone calls, which by now was beginning to snowball. It was only when the scale of his correspondence became apparent that Nick finally began to appreciate fully just what a huge problem alcoholism is. Nick, thinking like the entrepreneur he is, swung into action. He decided to seize the moment, and throw himself totally into helping drunks and their families. That meant putting his help service and day centres on a more formal basis.

Nick and Kelly had subsidised the centres all through their days on the Northern Club circuit. Teresa, who joined them in 1980 and who, like Kelly had never drunk to excess, also became committed to the cause. With the demise of the club circuit in 1983, all three continued their support of the centres using income from their involvement with boxing, the 'glamour' industry, and theatrical publicity. As we have seen, in the late 'eighties Teresa even went to work for a car rental company when things got particularly tight.

They set up their day centres wherever they could find suitable, preferably free, accommodation. When none was available they used their own home in Hounslow; it was common for bunk beds to fill their living space. As Nick's services became better known among the local drunks, these times in Hounslow became highly problematic. Well-disposed neighbours would often join the cause and put up 'members' when the house overflowed.

It was during one of these desperate periods that Nick mentioned his problems to Dr. David Marjot in one of their regular telephone calls. Dr. Marjot told Nick that there were empty buildings on his hospital estate that were falling into disrepair. They had become a major problem to the hospital authorities because rat infestations had turned them into a health risk.

The authorities were planning a major redevelopment, however, because many of the buildings were 'listed' as being of architectural significance, they could not be demolished and the land used for new hospital buildings, nor could they be sold for redevelopment to raise funds, at least not without a long and drawn out bureaucratic process. The buildings were just left there, slowly rotting.

Nick decided to pop down to the hospital and take a look for himself. The first person he saw was dressed in an ill-fitting suit, standing motionless, and ear pressed tightly against the wall. A bemused Nick was beckoned over, and he too stood there, ear pressed against the stonework, listening carefully. "I can't hear a thing," said Nick. "Neither can I," said his new friend. "It's been like that all day." So it was, that a soon-to-be neighbour from the nearby psychiatric ward was the first to welcome Nick to his future clinic.

Not put off by this eccentric introduction, Nick immediately saw the potential of the run-down site. His "I can do that" mentality went into overdrive; he convinced Dr. Marjot to arrange an appointment with the hospital authorities. The authorities themselves were not particularly interested one way or the other, but they were finally convinced by Nick's sales patter that they should hold a further meeting where they "would possibly consider allowing him the use of one particular building on the St Bernard's site." It had been the geriatric ward of the psychiatric wing of the hospital, and was in a dreadful condition.

Despite Dr. Marjot's wholehearted support, many in the hospital's management were not totally convinced of the merits of handing the building over to Nick.

However, Nick won them over one by one. In a social chat before a formal meeting, Nick discovered that one of the objectors was a keen football fan, and had been unable to get tickets for the upcoming International match at Wembley. "I can do that." If Nick could get the tickets, he reckoned his chances of leasing the ward would be vastly improved.

There were no promises, but a little good will couldn't hurt. With all his contacts in the sport and entertainment business it took only a few phone calls to get the tickets. It proved to everyone involved that Nick had the knack of making things happen, and soon he had the hospital's agreement on the move.

The local newspaper ran the story about Nick Charles setting up his new day centre prior to his first day. When he turned up on that Monday morning to survey his new domain he found the lawn outside the building crowded with people.

"Who are you?" Nick asked innocently.

"We're the drunks," he was told.

"Good. So let's get to work."

The ward finally placed at their disposal was truly disgusting. The smell of incontinent geriatrics pervaded the whole building. Nevertheless, the drunks on work therapy soon had the site cleared of both rats and odours, and after a fortnight, what turned out to be the last Nick Charles day centre was fully operational.

Why the last Nick Charles day centre? Although the ward had been abandoned, its telephone was still operational. Nick agreed to pay the phone bill in order to have contact with the outside world via the hospital switchboard. However, the telecommunications manager of the hospital refused to recognise the Nick Charles day centre, instead insisting that incoming callers must ask for the Chaucer Ward, it's official name; all the wards in the hospital had been named after famous writers. The pompous 'jobsworth' also refused to use the term 'clinic' because Nick had no medical qualifications, despite the input and active support of committed professionals like Dr. Marjot.

Just to be awkward, the officious official also refused to allow the use of the term 'day centre,' even with Nick's name dropped from its title. Ever the pragmatist, Nick decided: "Let's waste no more time on this nonsense. From today we're called 'Chaucer!' Not 'day centre.' Not 'Clinic.' Not 'Ward.' Just 'Chaucer.' Now let's get on with our work."

Nick still chuckles at how an almost insignificant implement, like a telephone, could play such a pivotal role in his life. For not only was it the reason behind the name Chaucer, but also it was on that very phone that Teresa received the fateful call from Glasgow. From the moment she answered that phone call Chaucer ceased to be a day centre, and became a de-facto fully-fledged clinic.

8

Chaucer is Born

In September 1989 Nick moved his day centre from his house in Livingstone Road, Hounslow to the Chaucer Ward of St. Bernard's Hospital, Southall, Middlesex. The ward had been abandoned - in a hurry. Patients had been moved out, leaving their unmade beds, complete with soiled pillows and sheets. Property was scattered all around, including bits of clothing, half-smoked packs of cigarettes; there was even a set of false teeth in a glass at one bedside.

The building had holes all over the roof, through which the rain poured in. There was no electricity and no water, but for some odd reason the central heating supplied by the steam from the hospital's boiler room was still working. It didn't take long for the local dossers to discover this was a snug place to crash. Not the most house-proud of the human race, it took the down-and-outs only a few weeks to completely trash the place.

The hospital authorities were intent on demolishing the site and redeveloping it, but that was going to take a long time, given the complexity of local planning regulations. They had a problem! Their financially motivated inattention was spawning an interim health hazard very close to the hospital.

Consequently, there was little objection to Nick and his day centre moving in to Chaucer on condition that he would leave the site when redevelopment began. Nick readily agreed to this proviso; he had accepted similar conditions many times before, after all beggars can't be choosers. He would move out on request, but Nick's character meant that he wouldn't concern himself with that particular problem until the next moving day arrived.

Lucky 13

Into this chaos came the third of the trio of women who would
eventually dominate Nick's life. In 1989 Kelly and Teresa were
joined by Nikki de Villiers, although the two original female
members of Nick Charles Enterprises wouldn't come to recognise
this fact for another year. When Nikki was first introduced to Nick
in the summer of 1989 she was a bigger wreck than the Chaucer
building. Nikki had been degraded and brutalised all her life; her
torments have been graphically portrayed in her biography: *Nikki
... all about secrets.*

From a very young age she had been both physically and sexually
abused. The most vicious of her tormentors was her father, a self-
confessed murderer, who also took pleasure in killing Nikki's
pets. Like so many victims of callous paedophiles, Nikki blamed
herself for her predicament. Then in her teens, almost inevitably,
she sought solace in the bottle, but this only made things worse.
Although managing to keep herself in employment, Nikki, a soon-
to-be alcoholic in support of her habit, found herself adrift among
the pond life: a vicious, sordid and violent group of characters
with no conscience and no shame. Nikki had to live on her wits,
but those wits were addled by alcohol. She was beaten up and
raped on a number of occasions, and being shunned by normal
society there was no one to turn to for protection. This all
reinforced her sense of worthlessness, guilt and hopelessness. The
consequent self-loathing led inexorably on to self-mutilation and
suicide attempts. Her sporadic pathetic attempts at sobriety
would always end in binges as she tried to escape her horrors by
drinking herself into oblivion. In her early thirties, it was only a
matter of time before she succeeded in killing herself, either deliberately or accidentally.

Through a twist of fate Nikki was taken to Nick's day centre. But
it wasn't easy, and it wasn't nice. A basket case of self-pity and
self-disgust in equal measure, she wasn't the easiest of patients.
Nick would start to believe he was getting somewhere with her
treatment, and then Nikki would flip, and spiral downward with
venomous outpourings of self-hatred and a destructive aversion
to anyone and everyone trying to help. After all, who would want
to help such a despicable person? Nick would be driven to distraction. He would scream and shout at her; on one occasion amid
Nikki's screaming threats to slash her wrists, he even threw her a

packet of razor blades and told her to get on with it. But he pressed on, and through a mixture of cajoling and bullying, carrot and stick, after a number of false starts, Nikki finally climbed aboard the wagon at 11.50pm on September 22, 1989 and she has been sober ever since. Nikki, proved to be the first of the many successes of Chaucer.

Everyone needs a crutch in the early days of his or her sobriety, and Nikki was no exception. In order to support her resolve she decided to hang around Nick, and around the security of Chaucer. Nikki would do anything - and she meant anything - to be allowed to stay. All Nick asked from her was to take a mop and bucket, and join the group of drunks cleaning the building. And there was a lot of cleaning to do, now that the first job, that of fixing the roof, had been completed in the first week of occupation. The roof damage had been superficial; all it needed was money to put it right. Nick had been sending out begging letters to anyone and everyone he could think of. Pete Townshend of The Who came through with the cash; this wouldn't be the last time that the rock star came to the rescue in Chaucer's struggle for existence.

Now that the rain no longer poured in, the task of making the building habitable began in earnest. That job made Hercules' chore of cleaning the Augean stables look like child's play. The ward itself had to be gutted, the floors and walls replaced, and then the whole building redecorated. There was no shortage of projects for work therapy! But before any of this could start, the whole area had to be decontaminated. For the first time in her life Nikki felt needed and appreciated; and she really was needed. Nikki led the clean-up gangs from the front, and so Nick put her in charge of the thirty plus volunteers. She is still leading from the front, eventually becoming the General Manager of Chaucer. Nikki, an exemplar of the indomitable human spirit, is an inspiration to everyone at the Clinic.

Ask Nikki what her lucky number is, and she will tell you: thirteen. That was the number of human turds she found on the luckiest day of her life, the day she was given responsibility for leading the first clean sweep of the building, the day she knew she had a future. There was excrement everywhere, on windowsills, in the bedding, on the floor. As she says without a hint of irony: "I hope the s**t came from the dossers, and not the patients in the geriatric ward, if only for the geriatrics' sake!" Nick, with his alcoholic's experience of psychiatric wards, which tended to be jammed full of unwanted elderly patients, wasn't convinced.

It took them two full weeks to decontaminate the building. In the first sweep of the building they got rid of the rats and threw out all the rubbish, but an all-pervading stench remained. They resorted to squirting industrial strength disinfectant over every square inch: floors, walls, doors, windows and ceilings. In total they used over fifty gallons of the stuff. The building then had to be hosed down after the application. Problem! The derelict building that housed Chaucer had no supply of running water, and so they improvised. There were plenty of willing hands to carry buckets, and for the really big job of washing the place down after it was disinfected their solution was to attach fire hoses to the nearest hydrant and drench everything. Luckily the central heating was still functioning, so they turned on all the radiators and the building soon dried out.

Leaning on a Lamp-post

However, their real problem was the lack of electricity because, when darkness fell, everything had to stop. Winter was approaching fast and, with the dark nights drawing in, something had to happen - and quickly. Lack of this essential service was standing in the way of both treatment and renovation work. However, help was at hand from among the original fifteen drunks who stood on the lawn that first Monday morning when the Chaucer day centre opened for business. A few weeks into the work, with the roof on, and the renovation in full swing, Nick had spotted Bill among the helpers. He was easily identifiable, shuffling around in his London Electricity Board donkey jacket: a memento of past employment.

Within two days of being asked, Bill had connected the electricity supply, but mysteriously it worked only during the hours of darkness. "It comes on automatically from a timer switch," Bill said knowledgeably.
"What time is that?" asked Nick.
"Can't tell you exactly," said Bill "but my best guess is you'll have power from just before dusk until around dawn." It was quite a few weeks before Nick solved the mystery of the erratic source of

electricity. However, he was soon to discover why the original power supply had been cut off from Chaucer: the hospital had deliberately broken the connection as a safety precaution when they first abandoned the ward to an invasion of dossers. The workings of a huge hospital bureaucracy run exceedingly slow, but eventually someone realised that the now reoccupied ward was without electricity.

The big day arrived for the electricity to be reconnected. Bang! All the fuses blew. They were replaced. Bang! They blew again. Whatever Bill had done to the wiring was causing a huge power surge that blew out the fuse-box. Bill's handiwork had to be reversed. However, the innovative Bill had by now fallen off the wagon and quietly disappeared. The word went out to all the Chaucer Marauders in the area: find Bill! Only he could untangle the rat's nest of cable connections joining Chaucer to the outside world, and Nick, by now highly suspicious of Bill's handiwork, didn't want the hospital looking too closely into their novel power supply of the past few weeks.

A few hours later a couple of Marauders tracked Bill down to a local park, drinking rotgut with a large crowd of other tramps. Extricating an unwilling semi-conscious wino from among his aggressive fellows without suffering violent retribution takes a psychology unique to street-wise ex-alcoholics. Just grabbing him was out of the question, and so the Marauders hatched a plan. They told Bill's drinking mates that he was to receive a £20,000 legacy from his aunt in Florida, who had recently died. But first, quite reasonably, he had to be sobered up, so that he could collect the money. To the collective logic of a gang of drunks, a £20,000 legacy for one is £20,000 worth of booze to be shared amongst them all. Consequently, far from protecting Bill, the gang rushed to squeeze him into a supermarket trolley - there's always a supermarket trolley around homeless drunks - and they helped wheel him the two miles to Chaucer!

Slowly, very slowly, Bill sobered up, and it was only then that Nick found out that Chaucer had been connected directly into the circuit that lit the streetlight positioned just outside the hospital's West Gate. The exploding fuses were only to be expected, since two separate power sources were simultaneously feeding the electric circuitry in Chaucer.

Nick tried to talk Bill into disconnecting the wiring, but he refused. In his addled state he refused to touch the lamp-post without wearing his official jacket; only authorised London Electricity Board workers could touch lamp-posts! In the rush to get him to Chaucer, the Marauders had accidentally discarded his pride and joy, his LEB jacket, in the park; he would never see it again. Nick's immediate solution was to whisper to a nearby Marauder to find any spare donkey jacket lying around, and stencil the words London Electricity Board on the back.

Bill was presented with his Lectric Bored (!) coat, but as spelling wasn't one of his strong points either, he didn't notice the mistakes. Believing himself to be LEB authorised once more, Bill happily went off to unhook the counterfeit cables. Chaucer was finally connected to a twenty-four hour a day legitimate power supply.

Unfortunately this fairy story didn't end happily ever after. The Marauders forgot to tell Bill the story about his aunt from Florida and the £20,000 legacy. The next time Bill staggered into his drunken pals in the park he was savagely beaten up; his punishment for squandering their money 'on the piss.'

Powerful Cut

However reconnection didn't end their electrical problems. During the first six months of Chaucer's life, intermittent power cuts were occurring on a regular basis. The inescapable fact was that the place badly needed re-wiring. The problem was that this particular job required a special main core cable, but the cost was prohibitive. However, without the re-wiring Chaucer would not pass an official inspection. By now, after his falling out with the drunks in the park, Bill was long gone, and so Nick was on the lookout for another trained electrician.

The jungle drums started beating among the drunks, and the word soon got out to the other addiction units in the area that the newly occupied Chaucer was in desperate need of an electrician. By that time the manner in which 'members' helped Nick refit the Clinic was also becoming well known throughout the local medical community, and not just among the drunks. Consequently the nearby hospitals would occasionally ring him up and say: "Do you need a plumber?" or "a bricklayer?"

Nick recalls one occasion when Dr. Marjot's secretary called him to ask if Chaucer needed a carpenter. The Clinic was full, and anyway they already had a carpenter. "He's also a plumber." Chaucer had a plumber in residence. Nick was distracted by the mumbled conversation going on in the background. "What about a plasterer?" The Clinic's walls were in pristine condition. "A bricklayer?"

Nick quipped: "He's not a salesman by any chance?" Immediately the voice of John Linton shouted out the magic words, "I can do that," over the phone. Laughing at this total stranger using his catch-phrase, Nick agreed to take John on for a week until alternative arrangements could be made. Fourteen years on, John Linton, an original Chaucer Marauder, is still with them: a corner stone of the Clinic's staff.

However, John's arrival didn't solve Nick's electrical problems. Then one fateful day the alcoholism unit of St. Bernard's, just down the road from Chaucer, called to say: "We have a drunk electrician on detox here. His name is Jim. Is he any use to you?" and luckily he agreed to transfer to Chaucer. Luckily? Jim was unaware of the true state of the building; otherwise it is doubtful he would have been so quick to move. Yet move he did. The rewiring problem was half-solved.

The other half was solved less than a month later when an enormous wooden reel bearing thick core cabling arrived on a low-loader. The delivery note, tucked into a polythene pouch and tacked onto the reel, simply read 'Chaucer Clinic/Paid in Full.' All the driver wanted was a signature, so that he could be on his way. A baffled Nick said he hadn't ordered any cabling. The driver said it wasn't his problem. All he wanted was a name on the piece of paper to say that he had dropped it off, and he would be on his way. Jim, the electrician, suddenly appeared at Nick's side. "Oh good, it's arrived." He signed the docket, and set off to supervise the re-wiring. Not for the last time would Nick whisper to himself: "Don't ask!"

Marauders in Hot Water

As winter set in it got even colder. The steam central heating was still in fine working order, but of all things Chaucer's immersion heater finally decided to give up the ghost. Then, early one

Wednesday morning, things began to look up. Ray, a central heating engineer who was a 'member,' suddenly appeared carrying a second-hand water heater. He fitted it with a minimum of fuss, and quietly took the old heater away. Nick thanked both Ray and Chaucer's newly appointed Business Manager, Teresa Weiler, for sorting out the problem. Teresa was confused. She had no idea where the heater had come from, and made a note to quiz Ray later. However, that would have to wait since she and Nick were expected at the hospitality suite of the nearby hospital, where they were to attend the goodbye party for a friendly consultant.

They entered the suite to find an almost hysterical private secretary telling everyone that the celebrations would have to be cancelled. Their hot water system had failed. He asked Nick if there was anyone at Chaucer who was capable of fixing water heaters? On inspecting the wall mounted heating system, Nick commented "that's lucky, it's the same model as ours at Chaucer." What he didn't notice were the dents and scratch marks that were uncannily similar to those on the heater they had so recently discarded! Nick went straight to the 'phone. "Hello Ray, it's Nick here, the water heating system has broken down in the hospitality suite. Can you come over and fix it?"

There was a long pause before "Yeah! Well that depends ... on whether you want the hot water up here, or down there!" Nick quickly put two and two together. Now he knew where the heater had come from, and also where the old heater had gone. So he quietly replaced the receiver, and returned to tell the secretary that unfortunately Ray had gone off for the day.

The Sultan's Peacock

Although payments from the Department of Health and Social Security (DHSS) were delivering a regular and substantial cash flow, over and above Chaucer's present requirements, Nick was concerned that the support would not be permanent. Should the state reduce its commitment, the hand-to-mouth funding, sufficient to keep the day centres going, couldn't keep a residential centre afloat, with its longer-term commitments. As head of a Charity, Nick decided to go looking for charity. Having only recently received an official registration, Nick, somewhat naively, thought that the donations would come flooding in.

Unfortunately not everyone was as forthcoming as Pete Townshend. It wasn't long before Nick realised that helping alcoholics cope with their self-inflicted problems couldn't compete with heart-rending pictures of starving children, abused animals, lifeboats, cancer research, or even politically correct and 'fashionable' causes like AIDS. Chaucer found itself at the wrong end of a long line of outstretched hands; but stretch out his hand he did.

Nil desperandum! Nick decided that he would approach the problem in a constructive and organised way. He identified 500 organisations in West London and decided to send out an appeal for financial help. There was only one problem: the cost of postage. He was delighted when an unemployed accountant on detox at the Clinic offered to get his wife to pay for the stamps. She had a top job with a local delicatessen supplier and could afford it. A week later Nick had a visit from the security staff of the wife's company. She had posted the 500 letters as promised, but she had processed them through her office's franking machine, and unfortunately one of the appeals had been addressed to ... the very same delicatessen supplier. Whoops!!

However, if plan A doesn't work, try plan B. Nick mused that since charity begins at home, he would start there and gradually work outwards, particularly since his next-door neighbour was the world's richest man. For across a sports/recreation field was the 'Aviary,' the English country home of the Sultan of Brunei. So, like a good neighbour, Nick naively thought he would just phone to say hello, and acquaint the Sultan with the work at Chaucer.

Nick realised that he was unlikely to talk directly to the Sultan at the first attempt, but he should at least get through to the aide-de-camp. What he got was an assistant's assistant's assistant, a long way down the pecking order. As for the right-hand man: "Sorry he's a bit tied up at the moment, so he can't come to the phone." Despite several further attempts, he got no further, and each time the right-hand man was constantly "a bit tied up at the moment."

Then one sunny afternoon a peacock wandered nonchalantly into the Chaucer grounds, causing chaos among a work-therapy group at a hairdressing class. They tried to shoo it away, but it stubbornly refused to leave. The group leader promptly took the cape from around the shoulders of a half-shorn client, slipped it over the bird's head and secured it with the ties, thus preventing the bird from escaping. It was carried unceremoniously, hissing and kicking, into the drug room, and the door was locked.

Nick phoned the hospital to ask for advice, and was told: "it probably belongs to the Sultan." At last, a chance to get through to the aide-de-camp! Not wasting a moment, Nick called the Aviary about the peacock: "So that's how the house got its name!" Once again he was told that: "the ADC was a bit tied up at the moment."

However, at the mere mention of the capture of the valuable bird Nick was put straight through to the man himself. Surely a handsome reward was on the cards! With not a single word about the peacock, Nick went straight into his patter about his new charity, and asked for the correct address in Brunei to send an appeal to the Sultan.

"Can we see the bird please?" The ADC ignored Nick's persistent references to the financial plight of his charity. "I will come personally to collect it straight away!"

"No you can't come just yet." Nick wanted to make a good impression with the potential donor; apart from needing to untie the bird and get it out of its captive cell in the drug room, he wanted time to compose a begging-letter that would be handed over along with the bird.

"Why can't I come over straight away to pick up the bird?" was the somewhat suspicious reply.

Quick as a flash Nick replied, "because he's a bit tied up at the moment." Chuckling to himself, Nick the comedian just couldn't stop himself from delivering the punch line. Not knowing Nick's sense of humour, the ADC took the joke for sarcasm. Being sarcastic is not a good tactic when you're trying to squeeze money out of someone! Later that day Nick handed over the peacock, and more in hope than expectation, the begging-letter.

Unsurprisingly, Chaucer never did get the donation; to this day the Sultan is totally unaware of his neighbours. The peacock still turns up for a visit every so often, but now Nick tells everyone to leave it alone and it usually finds its own way home. The bird sometimes even brings along a friend. On two separate occasions a heron from the 'Aviary' ate every goldfish in Chaucer's ornamental pond; Nick no longer restocks it.

Hush, Hush Sweet Charlotte

As Nikki began settling in, and taking on more and more responsibilities, she began to see herself as indispensable to Nick. She really didn't like the idea of Teresa being around. That Teresa had been with Nick for over a decade, and wasn't a drunk, just reinforced the resentment. Still not fully over the booze, Nikki got it into her head that she loathed the "middle-class snooty la-de-da b**ch." This antagonism soon escalated into an 'either her or me' situation.

Teresa, meanwhile was totally unaware of the growing hatred, and was doing her best to help Nikki.

When Nikki confronted Nick with her demands, he told her to talk to Teresa and sort things out. Nikki stormed into Teresa's office saying that she hated her and couldn't work with her. She knew that Teresa would never leave Nick and Chaucer, so the only option open to her was to kill herself! The booze was still doing Nikki's thinking, despite her being sober for some time; Nick has always taught that alcoholism is a form of insanity.

As calm and unflustered as ever, Teresa said she was sure they could work out their differences. Nikki should think the situation over and come back in forty-eight hours when they would talk again. She returned after two days to find Teresa presenting her with Charlotte, a King Charles spaniel puppy. The ice had been broken, and as Nikki moved further along the road of sobriety, she found herself starting to like Teresa, so that today they are the best of friends.

Then came the dreadful day when Charlotte disappeared; Nikki was inconsolable. The Clinic was searched from top to bottom, but with no success. One of the searchers, Sean O'Rafferty, sauntered up to Nick and mumbled. "I 'eard some o' d'guys sayin' dat da dog cost 250 quid. 'Cos dat's a lotta money." Then with a knowing wink he added "persons unknown could use 'er to breed pups." In his unsubtle way he was trying to help Nick, but he couldn't bring himself to 'grass' on his mates.

"The stupid beggars will need a bleedin' miracle," replied Nick. "She's been doctored!" Half an hour later Charlotte came trotting up the garden path.

Mission Impossible?

Nick's story had finally reached that point where, as much to his amazement as to everybody else's, Chaucer was up and running, and his team was coming together. "I never set out to create a clinic; I just wanted to run free day centres to help fellow alcoholics. Harry the Hat would have been amazed." It never occurred to Nick that he would one day be in charge of a residential treatment centre. He was only qualified as a drunk, and with no medical training; it just sort of ... happened. Chaucer crept up on him unawares. But once it had happened it didn't take him long to see the incredible opportunity. In a clinic built by alcoholics for alcoholics and run by alcoholics, Nick could do far more good than would have ever been possible with his day centres alone, and certainly more than some other alcohol units run by doctors who themselves drink too much.

"At last," I thought, "we have finally reached a point in our conversations where I can start asking Nick in detail about his approach to business, rather than just listening to his anecdotes. Maybe at last I'll find out what makes him tick. Finally I'll get some solid case material for my lectures." It seemed to me that, thus far in Nick's entrepreneurial career, there had been no strategic direction in his thinking. He had been sleepwalking on a random path from one spontaneous money-making scheme to the next; an approach that had, almost by accident, turned his loss-making private charity, the day centres supported by his ad-hoc income as a freelancing entrepreneur, into a formally registered not-for-profit business funded by the state. However, now that the health authorities were paying for treatments, they would insist that the whole enterprise be put on a far more organised footing. The up-side was the creation of Chaucer and a guaranteed income (although not in the long-term); but the downside was the need to jump through their bureaucratic hoops.

With the DHSS looking over his shoulder Nick had to be far more business-like in his commercial dealings. I wanted to know about the original business plan for Chaucer and the various other documents produced to keep the bank manager happy. What procedures did he put in place to develop more general and on-going plans for the future? Where did Nick go for business advice? What administrative systems did he put in place? Did he know what was expected of him now he was a reputable businessman responsible for a Charity rather than a freewheeling entrepreneur? Was the business literature any use to him? What books did he read?

Following this torrent of questions, I began explaining to Nick a range of business concepts, the standard stuff I teach to my students, like value chains, supply chains, customer resource management, product life cycles, balanced score cards, etc. etc. Did Nick use any of these concepts? Maybe, I asked, since Nick was a natural, he used these ideas unawares, simply because they seemed obvious to him. Nick's answer was immediate: "None of the above. Both I, and all of those around me, just did what was sensible at the time." Even a dozen years after founding Chaucer, these questions about the world of formal business procedures still leave Nick nonplussed.

At the end of one particular session I started explaining how most large companies promote stories about founders/senior executives as part of a bonding process for employees; I gave Nick examples of such corporate mythologies from Honda and Hewlett-Packard. I went on to explain how a major requirement of the bonding process is the development and ritual application of company visions and mission statements that are meant to encapsulate the essence of what the company is, what it does, how it does it, and where it is going. I even dug out a few annual reports to show Nick real examples from both private and public sectors. Had Nick produced a clear mission statement for Chaucer so that his colleagues understood what was expected of them?

"Do you mean to tell me that employees take this stuff seriously? You're having me on! I've never heard of anything so fatuous and daft in my life. It's a joke surely? What you've shown me are just strident wish-lists of phoney superlatives; self-congratulations for things not yet achieved." When I convinced him that companies really did take this stuff very seriously, and that they spent a great deal of time and money developing their missions and visions, Nick's response was immediate. "It seems to me that these state-ments are just more of your lamp-posts; support for businessmen and women who don't know what they are doing, and who have to convene meetings in a vain attempt to find out? If you really want to inspire your people then by all means have a punchy slogan, but not a self-conscious almost smug set of paragraphs that are these mission statements. We do have a slogan at Chaucer: 'The hell ends here!' - and that's sufficient bragging about the future."

"Do I have a mission? Of course I have a mission! 'I help drunks to get off the booze!' But I don't need to write down that simple sentence for everyone to know what I, and my colleagues at Chaucer are all about. I wouldn't dream of sticking any mission statement on a board outside the Clinic, because there's no point in stating the self-evident."

"Do I have a vision? Of course I do! I have hopes for the future; ambitions, dreams for the future. But will the future end up exactly that way? Of course not! My vision helps me formulate my actions in order to achieve my goals. But it can never be a clear image of the future. I saw more than enough hallucinations when I was a drunk, to have any truck with that nonsense now I'm sober. My vision is nebulous; I certainly couldn't express it explicitly in words - for that would castrate its vitality. Furthermore, mine is a vision for the future, and not of it. I try to change my future to advantage, but would never delude myself that I am in control of that destiny. I'd never go looking for certainty because it simply isn't there; I wouldn't waste my time trying to control the dynamic uncertainty. I take each day as it comes, and act appropriately in pursuit of my vision: 'Sufficient unto the day is the evil thereof.' (Matthew 6:34)"

"However, what I will accept is that my anecdotes are a ready-made mythology for Chaucer, and that they are a powerful cohesive force for the Clinic. It's funny! I thought it was just my extrovert personality and the residue of my show-business days. Until you told me about corporate myths I never thought of my storytelling in this way, but now you explain it, creating a mythology is exactly what I was doing. Perhaps subconsciously I could see the benefits."

It began dawning on Nick that, in his inadvertent creation of a mythology for himself and Chaucer, he had also stumbled on a surprising educational benefit. For following his example, Chaucer members would recount their own stories, their own mythologies. And in those stories, like Nick, they were heroes and not victims. They were at the centre of events and not at the margin. They were taking control of their own destinies. Suddenly they had rediscovered a pride in themselves, and in doing so took a major step on the road to sobriety.

So I had convinced Nick over the value of Mythology, but missions and visions? From his standpoint it's far better to have a considered and realistic understanding of what he actually does. This helps him recognise problems as they come along. "Personally, I know what I'm doing, why I'm doing it, and how I'm doing it; but that's totally different from the way in which I do it, namely running the business that administrates and facilitates the doing. I've always separated 'the business I'm in' from 'doing the business' , and I strive to get the balance right between the two. The 'business I'm in,' namely the health business, is totally outside of my control." The regulations are set externally, and Nick realises that he has to conform to these requirements and run Chaucer with administrative probity; or rather Teresa runs that side for him.

Furthermore, Nick knows there must be a strong discipline among staff and members, and he leaves that to Nikki. Furthermore, he recognises that Chaucer can only work if it remains a caring and humane environment: Kelly keeps an eye on that. His three ladies don't need vision and mission statements either. They too know the what, why and how of their roles. If there is a vision and mission, it is there for all to see, encapsulated in their actions rather than in their words. As for everyone else in the Clinic, both members and employees, open doors to himself, Kelly, Teresa and Nikki, prove a far more effective mode of communication of what they are about, than do a lifeless group of sentences.

"Furthermore, our policy for employing carers at the Clinic is that they must have been alcoholics who have recovered at Chaucer. You could say they have gone through an apprenticeship with us, and consequently they know what our present members are going through. Our carers know from personal experience that our programme works; and that's far more effective than a mission

statement." I personally observed that this employment policy
had the extra benefit that the ex-drunks on the staff had "been
there, done that," and so are not phased by the sometimes truly
disgusting, sometimes terrifying behaviour of new members.

As for Nick's role, he just does the business. He makes things
happen, and that takes a very special skill: having a very clear
idea of what, why and how he is doing what he is doing - namely
helping drunks. This what, why and how takes up all his waking
hours; he doesn't want to waste time developing missions and
visions, or thinking about keeping the business viable, or
planning for hazards and opportunities that haven't happened
yet. Unknown and unknowable hazards inevitably crop up, but
Nick has faith in the abilities of both himself and of those around
him. He knows that something will always turn up that will
enable him to deal with whatever comes his way. But his isn't a
blind faith. There are always opportunities. Those who think
opportunities are scarce simply don't understand the notions of
risk and enterprise: a heady mix of opportunity and hazard. Nick
would never seek to avoid risk. He just gets stuck in. He is clear
that opportunities and hazards are everywhere, and so he goes
out looking for opportunities, or at the very least he is ready for
them when they happen. As for the hazards, his trick is to recognise them early and find ways of avoiding them. Dealing with risk
means treating each moment, each situation on its own merits.

I slowly began to realise that Nick's anecdotes, far from being
some sanitised version of a mis-remembered past, do in fact hold
the essence of his pragmatic approach. For his stories differentiate
between what is relevant and irrelevant, between what is appropriate and inappropriate, simply by being there and by living each
moment. He refuses to waste his time pushing pieces of paper
around, playing the role of the businessman who is deluding
himself that he is preparing his company for a future imperfect.
Nick sticks to the purpose behind why he is in the sobriety
business in the first place. He insists that this must transcend mere
financial, regulatory and administrative niceties. Cash flow,
regulations and administrative processes aren't allowed to interfere in any way with his more important purpose. For otherwise,
why should he bother?

"So you know what you can do with your mission statements!"

9

Even Drunks can be Capitalists

There we have it! Nick doesn't believe in vision and mission statements; but neither does he have an arbitrary approach to 'doing the business.' So what exactly does he do at the Clinic? He helps drunks recover!

Why don't I drink?

Who better to answer a question that has perplexed me for many years: why, despite all the social pressures, am I adamant in refusing alcohol? I often joke that this is because of my upbringing in South Wales, surrounded as I was by a non-conformist denunciation of the devil's brew - I may have lost the religion, but I've kept the bigotry!

Nick's response was that I was asking the wrong question. "The important issue is why do most people drink? Abstainers are a minority. They don't drink because they never started imbibing, for whatever reason; or they find they don't like the drink, or the drink doesn't like them; or they are recovered alcoholics (some of whom are resentful of social drinkers, while others are just pleased to be free.)"

"You must realise that at the beginning, drinking is a social act. Everyone in Britain will inevitably drift into the company of alcohol, because that is the predominant culture. Once in this inner world, social divisions, personal inequalities, inhibitions, and inadequacies are submerged in a shared sense of well-being, which denies all the ups and downs of the outer world - at first it's all up, and no down. Most enjoy the 'high' of this social utopia; others find they can hide from the horrors in their life. The lucky ones, I call them social drinkers, are not trapped by the good feeling, and can move easily between the two worlds. Indeed, they choose to go back to the harsh realities of the real world - they can take it or leave it, and if necessary cancel any planned alcohol-driven return to the pleasure gardens of an unending 'summer of wine and roses.'"

"However, for some there is no choice, no escape. They must keep drinking - the alternative is a return to the real world of ever deepening lows. But instead of the permanent high they seek in booze, they find the period of euphoria grows shorter and shorter, and they enter a vicious circle of indulging to excess. Eventually the highs disappear altogether, but they must keep drinking just to escape the hell of despair. Now dependent on booze, many manage to function, after a fashion; others drop out of society completely as full-blown alcoholics.

However, in abusing alcohol, they make a nuisance of themselves, and spoil the party for social drinkers. The drunks become an irritation, an embarrassment to every potential soul-mate among the communion of social drinkers. Rejected, alcohol abusers have a choice: either drown in an excess of booze-fuelled bitterness (alone, or in the company of others of their kind), or abstain totally, debarred from the amnesia/social euphoria they desire, and often furiously resentful of social drinkers."

"You do realise where this logic is leading?" I responded. "Social drinking is itself a type of anonymity, and so I am forced to infer that the issue of anonymity among those stimulated by alcohol is a problem, not a solution. So where does this leave Alcoholics Anonymous? My uninformed view of an AA meeting is of self-pitying drunks sitting in abstemious rows. Their ritualised anonymity only goes to reinforce their sense of worthlessness. Worse, it resonates as a faint echo of their drunken nights with lost packs of nameless ex-friends. Far from helping, this may make their denial of entry to the company of social drinkers even harder to bear. Consequently, anonymity can end up doing the exact opposite of what was intended."

Nick butted in: "you've got it exactly! Drunks seeking help from Alcoholics Anonymous may come to depend on AA meetings as an alcohol substitute. Instead of returning to the outer world, they hide inside a false community, another world within a world, one they can easily identify with, because of its similarity to that wonderful inner world of alcohol-fuelled anonymous friendships - a world where they crave to stay, but dare not. This is no way to find the dignity and sense of self-worth so necessary for returning to the outer world, free of any dependence."

With a twinkle in his eye, Nick added: "as for your persistent abstinence, let's face it Ian, you're just an anti-social individualist. You've never wanted to join any desensitized merry band. Indeed, the very thought of losing your grip on your personalised reality simply terrifies you."

I Did It My Way

I knew that Nick had tried, and failed, to find sobriety with Alcoholics Anonymous. I could now see why he was never completely convinced by their twelve-step programme. He felt that "short sharp lectures, whether AA, National Health Service (NHS) or otherwise, turn alcoholics into experts of the one liner that gives many reasons why they shouldn't drink again. It doesn't teach how to stop drinking, any more than a philosophy, profoundly written and rooted in a God, can work by attempting to apply it to those without one: AA welcomes atheists!"

"I used to arrive early to sit in the back row of selected meetings, surreptitiously passing around a bottle that I knew would be there, all the while clapping the loudest at exhortations to sobriety. Other times, I would arrive after the confessions, saturated with alcohol and seeking sobriety, just in time for the coffee and biscuits, where I knew I would meet up with fellow-travellers - back to the pack. Eventually I began to realise that there was a problem in my seeking out the society of other drunks. In my case, and for people like me, joining an inward-looking group of drunks would only serve to reinforce the craving for alcohol. I had to get away and make new friends among social drinkers, join their world albeit as a teetotaller. There must be no going back to a group of boozers where falling off the wagon was the norm."

Unlike with AA, Nick's philosophy is that once the cure is complete you must walk away and rejoin the human race, but on your terms, not those of the drink and the drunk. Furthermore, he is annoyed that skulking around in the pretence of anonymity only creates ignorance about a disease that should be brought out into the open. "When you're that far gone, everyone around you knows you're a drunk, whatever you like to pretend to yourself."

Consequently Nick set out to find his own alternative to AA's 12-step programme, and decided to help himself achieve sobriety. Having succeeded, he launched a personal crusade to help others, who like him, had also tried and failed at Alcoholics Anonymous. The programme that he finally developed teaches those drunks everything they need to know about alcohol and its effects, the role of associated legal and illegal drugs, but most importantly it answers vital questions AA does not, and it teaches them how to stop drinking. Although Chaucer has grown enormously in both size and sophistication over the past decade, the recovery programme at its core remains unchanged from when Nick first developed it for his own sobriety.

Nick's Four Part Programme

Nick's programme for recovery is set out in four parts. Following on from an initial detox, part one deals sensitively with each alcoholic's unique personal problems, with individually crafted support and advice. These problems are often the trigger to why the member drank to excess in the first place. For many, this part of the programme is the critical factor separating success from failure. It is often the hardest part of the course for the member, as the emotional, physical and mental scars of years of alcohol abuse are brought out into the open.

Nick says: "Alcoholics are like fingerprints. Superficially they all look the same, until you examine them closely, and then you see the differences. In forty-odd years, both drunk and sober, I have never come across two alcoholics alike. Consequently, one treatment for all is totally unrealistic." As a result, the first part of the Chaucer approach is based on a theme chosen with the individual in mind, and so it is adapted for, and responds to, unique individual needs, problems and requirements. Therefore, it can be damaging for the member to start the programme with some preconceived notion of how long recovery will take.

There will always be setbacks, and these can prove disastrous if members set themselves unreasonable targets. As a rough guide Nick believes it takes on average around one month's rehabilitation for every year the member was drinking alcohol to excess. The more this can be expedited in a residential programme, the more solid the foundations for an alcohol-free life. Naturally, it is also vital for some of the rehab to be spent in the community.

The second part of the programme is education. Members face a 26-week programme of lectures on all aspects of alcohol. In particular they will learn about the psychological and physiological damage that it causes. They are shown photographic evidence of cirrhosis of liver, where scar tissue stops the liver functioning; or foetal alcohol syndrome, where the baby of an alcoholic mother can be born blind and with retarded growth. They are told about 'Bottle Nose,' where alcohol raises the blood pressure so that it burst veins in the nose. The red-nose phenomenon apparent in many heavy drinkers is exemplified in the face of the 1930s American comedian W.C. Fields. However, alcohol doesn't just burst veins in the nose; veins in the brain are similarly destroyed, and this leads to the obliteration of brain cells, and causes hallucinations and personality change.

The third module is work therapy. Abstinence from alcohol for life requires incredible self-discipline, and the obvious benefit of this part of the programme is the learning of regular discipline. Members are required to sign in daily by a specific time, and to carry out a given task to the best of their ability within a reasonable timescale. Because of their addiction, many drunks haven't been in paid employment for a long time, and some never have. For others, like doctors, journalists, policemen, and publicans, their occupational lifestyle has contributed to their problems. Whatever the background, the third module requires everyone to discover and learn new skills. The beauty of the scheme is that it actively encourages creativity and new ideas, allowing members to (re)discover and develop a belief in themselves and their personal abilities. The overarching idea is to prepare members for a return to the human race, encouraging them to engage in paid employment, or at the very least in voluntary work.

The fourth and final part of Nick's programme offers a comprehensive range of pursuits and hobbies, mostly at weekends and during the evenings. On Mondays through Wednesdays, a minimum of one pursuit per evening must be attended. The purpose of this part is to teach members how to use constructively the leisure time they previously spent drinking. Members must learn the important lesson that it is possible to have a good social life without alcoholic drinks in their hands.

Collateral Damage

Such brain damage can lead to Wernicke's encephalopathy, Korsakoff's psychosis, and other diseases, the gory details of which are exposed to every member. The lesser-damaged members don't need to look in books for illustrations of such devastating effects; they are surrounded by textbook examples in the walking wounded of the Clinic.

Members are confronted constantly with the anaesthetic and amnesiac qualities of alcohol. Nick tells of a once famous rugby player who had 22 different bone-fractures, but didn't realise it until his detox at Chaucer. Only when the booze wears off does the physical (and psychological) pain hit. The player's earliest breaks, some two and three years old, had healed badly because they went unnoticed and hence unattended. Some bones, particularly in his arm and ankle, had to be re-broken so they could heal correctly.

This was a very unusual case. Not so the excruciating pain of withdrawal symptoms, which most addicts experience, and only another drink or a detox with medication can stop. Every addict dreads the times when no alcohol is available, and the inevitable agony that will have to be endured. Having gone through the pain barrier of a detox once and emerged the other side, surely the memory of such searing pain would stop the drunk ever going through it again? Not so. The body has a built-in ability to block out the memory of acute agony: a form of natural amnesia. This acts against the alcoholic; as the torture of withdrawal is forgotten, so the prospect of a 'pint' or a 'nip' becomes harmlessly inviting once more.

That is why, as part of the education programme, Nick insists that during their detox, each drunk must write down a record of their worst suffering during withdrawal. This is typed out, laminated, and placed somewhere safe ready for the next time the drunk feels the dangerous urge to drink, when he/she is told to relive the horrors. In the absence of a video recording of the nightmare experience, Nick believes this is the best deterrent on offer.

Members are warned about other psychological phenomena that can occur months after sobriety has been achieved. Nick is always willing to use his own embarrassing incidents as an illustration, such as when during his time as a 'showbiz' publicist/entrepreneur, over ten years into his sobriety, he was looking for a major backer for one of his schemes.

He had already signed up playwright Anthony Marriott (*No Sex Please We're British*) and film producer Ben Arbeid (*The Hireling*). The three partners set off to a business meeting with a large firm of Chinese accountants that had expressed an interest. Walking along Gerrard Street in London's Chinatown, they happened to pass a bin overflowing with rubbish. Nick dressed in a very expensive silk suit just couldn't stop himself. Something buried deep in his psyche switched back to his days on the streets.

Nick plunged an arm deep into the bin, and scrabbled around for the waste food among the garbage. He suddenly came to, and realised what he was doing. Nick shamefacedly withdrew his arm, his sleeve now smothered in the remnants of a discarded chop suey and sweet and sour dinner. His actions took a lot of explaining to his would-be (and soon to be ex-) business partners.

Strife on the Ocean Wave

Even non-existent partners have caused Nick grief. The detectives from the CID arrived at Nick's accountants just before lunch and were grateful for biscuits and a cup of tea. It had been a difficult day and 'they were not happy bunnies.' "Do the names Baxter or Spedding mean anything to you?" A yacht involved in a credit fraud, recently moored at Cannes in the South of France had disappeared, and these shadowy figures had slipped through their fingers. The only lead the police had was the name of the purchasing company, given to them as Chaucer Clinic Ltd.

The accountant was perplexed because no such company existed. Although Chaucer was the name of Nick's clinic, for various complicated reasons the company running the charity had been left with the totally different name under which it had been originally registered, long before Nick even knew of Chaucer's existence. Luckily for Nick, the fraudsters were ignorant of that fact.

It transpired that Messrs Baxter and Spedding, using a phoney credit card, had bought a second hand yacht from a boatyard at a Thameside village. It didn't help that Nick had recently moved into a house at Egham, within a mile of that boatyard. Worse, the miscreants were driving a Rolls Royce bearing the phoney licence plate A1 NCK. This was Nick's own personalised plate, which was legally displayed on his Jaguar Sovereign. Yet again Nick gets sucked into complexity without even trying.

Subsequently it was discovered that Spedding owned the company that supplied office sundries to the Clinic, and that is what gave him the idea of using Chaucer's name in the fraud. Unfortunately, for him, he didn't benefit from his crimes; he died a few weeks later from a heart attack. Nick could breathe again.

First Success and First Failure

The formalised education programme at Chaucer has evolved slowly since the very beginning of the day centres. In those early days Nick identified likely candidates and treated them one-to-one. There were meetings full of hysteria and aggression; he even took them to post mortems run by a friendly pathologist to show them livers destroyed by cirrhosis. His score was eight out of eight, and all are still sober to this day. However, once he became involved with the 'authorities,' he was told that such visits had to stop; they were just too shocking for the drunks. Never mind that alcohol was killing them; Nick mustn't assault their finer sensibilities. Undismayed Nick now uses photographs of the various alcoholic conditions to get the message across; it's not ideal, but it's the next best thing. Ever the opportunist, Nick has taken this constraint imposed on him and turned it into an opportunity. He now uses his expanding collection of photographic horrors to reach beyond the Clinic members and raise awareness of these problems in the wider community, by spreading the message on his web sites: www.chaucerclinic.com and www.addictionnetwork.co.uk.

Nick had to formalise his recovery programme because once Chaucer was up and running he found its scale, and the time constraints made it impossible to maintain his one-to-one sessions. That is how Nikki de Villiers, his final one-to-one client, came to call herself Chaucer's first member. However, since she wasn't paying for treatment, and although she certainly was

Chaucer's first success, strictly speaking the title of Chaucer's first fully paid-up member must go elsewhere. Unfortunately the redheaded lady who could claim that title turned out to be far less of a success. The 'Poison Dwarf,' as she soon became known to everyone at the Clinic (after the perjorative nickname given to the character Lucy Ewing, played by Charlene Tilton, in the television soap opera *Dallas*), had a temper as violent as her hair colour. She proved to be a troublemaker from the first moment she took up her place.

In the early days the paid-up members supported by the DHSS had to collect their giro cheques personally from the local Post Office, cash them, and on returning to Chaucer hand over the requisite amount. Nick and the gang were just learning the ropes, and their fledgling procedures were somewhat slack, to say the least. They trusted members to go unaccompanied to the Post Office, and they didn't have a weekly check on whether fees had been paid in full. Unaided, Teresa had to put together the Clinic's accounting procedures from scratch. A very organised lady, she didn't copy other people's systems, but set about finding out the legal requirements of the 'powers that be' - in business jargon, the obligatory 'outputs' - and set about creating systems to deliver them, along with what she thought sensible for the smooth running of the Clinic.

It wasn't long before Teresa imposed order, and she soon discovered that 'Poison' hadn't paid her dues for over three weeks. On being informed of this Nick immediately sent the diminutive redhead to cash her three outstanding giros at the local Post Office. And that was the last they saw of her! A week later the Clinic received a post-card from Tenerife bearing the cheeky message: "Wish you were here." In a fury Nick phoned her father only to be told, "well you're a charity aren't you!"

Paranoia

Nick learned that lesson the hard way. It was one that would recur over the coming years, which was never to expect gratitude from the drunks he was helping, or even from their families. The drunks, or their relatives come to Nick begging for help, pleading for mercy, in tears, desperate and at their wits end, bitterly criticising the 'system,' and in complete sympathy with him and his cause. However, when he succeeds in helping an alcoholic gain sobriety there are two types of reaction: either they love him for it, or they say "I did it all by myself." In failure they blame him - totally. They even say that Nick is the cause of their failing, either, due to their own inability to come to terms with the Chaucer treatment programme, or to Nick's refusal to change his cure to fit their personal whims. They turn like rats in a trap; their anger knows no bounds. Character assassination and verbal abuse become rife; their hatred is as intense and all consuming as it is inexplicable. It can spill over into attacks on other members' personal property, and frequently on the Clinic's windows and doors. Fixtures, fittings and ornaments are smashed, plants in the gardens trashed. Therapists have found their cars vandalised, and even had their homes attacked. Poison pen letters, nuisance phone calls, ridiculous threats of court action, and the enormous amount of time and money spent dealing with the nonsense, are all in a days work.

Such unwelcome attention could have easily led to paranoia in Nick and his staff. One day he was driving home along the A40, when in his rear-view mirror he noticed a Jaguar Sovereign, just like his own, driving close behind with its lights flashing. He took the first exit, but then drove straight back onto the main road. His tail did exactly the same manoeuvre, still flashing its headlights. Nick speeded up and drove on to M25, leaving at Junction 13 for Egham. The tail was still there. Very concerned by now, Nick had a trick up his sleeve. His route home took him past the Egham police station. He turned into the police car park and was about to rush in to request police help, when the Jaguar pulled alongside him. The window rolled down and its occupant called out: "I've been trying to attract your attention for miles, waiting for you to stop. My name's Nick James. Can I buy your personalised car number plate A1 NCK?" Years later Mr. James still keeps contacting Nick, each time the price gets higher. Nick has been tempted a few times, but he will only sell the plate when times get really tough at Chaucer.

More Successes

However, even though you're paranoid, they can still be out to get you. It's a dangerous game, helping alcoholics! Most people, less dedicated than Nick, would leave the drunks to it. However Nick is totally committed, and he knows that if the member shares that commitment then there is a good chance of success. As for taking credit for success, for Nick the success itself is sufficient. And there have been many successes. Successes like Beverley, now back with her husband, who brought her healthy bouncing baby girl to the Clinic, saying it wouldn't have been born without Chaucer.

Then there was Rodney, who had never held down any job during his whole adult (and drunken) life. Yet at the age of 34, and with alcohol induced brain damage, he climbed onto the wagon and found a job as a road sweeper in West London. Rodney took a real pride in being the Council's best road sweeper. All seemed to be going well until one autumn day when Nick met him on the High Street. He was stressed out, mumbling incoherently to himself. He couldn't cope. A high wind was blowing the rubbish he had just swept up, back in his face. Nick told him to sweep down wind, and he reclaimed his title of best road-sweeper.

Unlike Rodney, many of the members can think for themselves, and have learned to emulate Nick's talent for lateral thinking. Chaucer gets old settees by the hundreds, dumped from house clearances. They have no value because they cannot be used at Chaucer following regulations concerning inflammable materials. So why do the Marauders accept them? They rip them up and look for money 'lost down the back.' They never find less than £5 in a settee; once they found £50. Tony Stinton did some work in my house a while ago, and on returning to the Clinic, Nick asked him about his visit. His response: "When can we get our hands on his settee; there's at least a score (£20) in there!"

The First Big Problem

Despite the successes it didn't take long for the first major bureaucratic problem to arise. When the lady from Glasgow had given them a licence for three beds over the phone, she had asked to know the number of beds Chaucer could handle; she was told twenty. For that many Nick needed a licence as a Home from the Local Authority, which involved an inspection. Everything was fine, except for the fact that Chaucer was run by alcoholics for alcoholics; they didn't employ any qualified medical staff. Without doctors and nurses they were only allowed to hold a residential licence and to rehabilitate the clients, but they weren't allowed to undertake medical detoxification.

'Rehab' without a detox? There was no point! A detox was the first major function of the programme, and in most cases this involved medication. Furthermore, if Chaucer could undertake a 'rehab' only, then the local authorities wouldn't be sending Nick any customers. Did this mean that Chaucer had fallen at the first hurdle? Not if Nick Charles had anything to do with it! He set about finding an innovative scheme that would dig them out of the bureaucratic hole. It didn't take long; after a brief conversation with his friend, and Chaucer's guardian angel, Dr David Marjot, he came up with the answer. Nick was thinking back to all the awkward detox cases that he had sent to Dr Marjot while he was running the day centres. "What did you do with Bill? He had a detox, but he wasn't staying in a medical ward."

"He refused to come into hospital," Marjot said, "and so I arranged a community detox for him. This is the application of a regime of medication, such as a course of Librium, but performed in the community by a responsible adult (in Bill's case, his wife) in a safe homely environment, always provided a doctor believes it is safe for the patient."

Nick quickly put two and two together, and came up with six. "Chaucer is a homely environment. Officially you can't be more homely than a residential home! I'm responsible, so why can't I do the community detox here. Why can't Chaucer be a rehabilitation unit at which I perform community detoxes for the clients you have checked out previously?"

Dr Marjot's face cracked with an inscrutable smile. "Your scrap of cunning seems to fit the regulations. I'd better check to see if you've found a loophole that allows you to slip between the rules." And so it proved; Nick's plan was perfectly legal. They gave it a try on a number of alcoholics scrupulously cleared by Dr Marjot. At first there was a lot of noise from the authorities, but the good doctor kindly provided Nick with copies of the various relevant regulations and that quelled the social workers and other objectors. Soon the authorities began to realise that Nick was undertaking rehabilitations that included a detox for less than a third of the price elsewhere. They could save money! Not surprisingly it wasn't long before this approach was common practice all over the UK. However, because of the compensation culture and the jobsworths, it all ended in 2005.

Pharaoh's Tomb

Because the Chaucer project had little money in the early days, Nick's policy was to refurbish and recycle literally everything. Even his own office chair was rescued from a rubbish skip in Chiswick. The Clinic's reputation for furniture restoration soon spread far and wide. Nick wasn't surprised when he received a phone call from the Unit General Manager of the local Health Authority who was in the market for a new (preferably sumptuous) office chair. Apparently, pharaoh ants, the scourge of ancient hospital buildings, had been found infesting the upholstery of his old chair.

Nick, who had agreed to find a replacement at a reasonable price, didn't know at the time that the offending chair had originally been upholstered by another furniture restoration work therapy group - based in St Bernard's hospital psychiatric unit. One of their patients had been eating a jam sandwich as he was upholstering the chair, and inadvertently dropped it into the chair. The patient, not wanting to continue eating a sandwich covered in fluff and horsehair, and couldn't be bothered to fish it out, left it where it had fallen. After all, no one was likely to see it. Except, that is, for the malicious pharaoh ants, who congregated in their thousands for the sugar-rich feast.

"I need a new chair, like yesterday," he urged Nick. "I've had to throw my old one away." Nick popped straight down to the Chaucer furniture restoration work therapy group, and they informed him that it would be no problem. They had just rescued a suitable old chair from a nearby skip. In due course the hospital executive received his new chair, beautifully restored with material cannibalised from some old curtains discarded from his own office just the week before. He was delighted with his new possession, until a few months later he found that it too was infested by pharaoh ants. So he rang Nick, who agreed to find another replacement. Chaucer's furniture group reported to Nick that they had just acquired yet another suitable chair. It took some years before the absurd truth surfaced. The same old chair was being recycled. And with each cycle it had grown thicker and thicker, and less recognisable as subsequent upholstery materials were added. The offending sandwich has now long gone, eaten by generation of ants, and so have the pharaohs, in search of sandwiches new.

Cash Flow Crises

This wouldn't be the last time that Nick was to discover that the
left hand of the hospital authorities didn't know what their right
was doing. Less than two years prior to the closure of the geriatric
wards, the hospital had spent a fortune on parquet flooring for
some of the now-abandoned buildings. On one of his regular
forays around the grounds Nick spotted the flooring and asked if
he could buy the wooden blocks. Just to get rid of him he was told
he could have them for the nominal sum of a few pounds. The
work therapy group dug them out, polished all undamaged
blocks, and managed to sell them to a contractor as flooring for
£5000.

News of the successes of Nick's work therapy group soon spread.
The local hospital had problems with a leaking roof on one of
their outbuildings, and so they agreed a contract with Nick to re-
slate it. Not because they wanted to help the Chaucer programme,
but because Nick's team came cheap! It was agreed that Chaucer
was to receive half the money in advance, which was to be used to
purchase new slates and other material. The authorities would
pay the remainder on completion, which they expected would be
in around six weeks.

As usual Chaucer was going through a bad financial patch, so
Nick was forced to treat some of this money as an advance on the
payment for the job - just enough to tide them over. However, the
cash remaining would only buy slates for a third of one side of the
roof. Nick's plan was that, once out of the short-term cash flow
crisis, he would buy the remainder of the slates and quickly
complete the job. In the meantime it had to look as though the
workers were getting on with the job. Their plan was to slate a
quarter of one side of the roof, cover it with a tarpaulin (a requirement of the Health and Safety Executive), take off the newly fitted
slates, and then use those rescued for the next quarter in view.
Cover that with tarpaulin, and repeat the process.

For seven weeks the authorities could see the workers beavering
away on the roof. They didn't expect a quick job - they were
drunks working up there after all - and they consoled themselves
with the fact that drunks came cheap! However, Chaucer's cash
flow crisis just wouldn't go away; Nick was in a bind. With no
collateral, he could hardly go to the bank for a loan. As a last

resort he telephoned Pete Townshend (of the Who) - the same Pete who paid for Chaucer's roof. Nick explained the situation, and asked for a loan of £1000. Tickled by this latest escapade, Pete sent the cheque, but as a donation; he said it was worth it for the entertainment value. They finished the roofing in three weeks, and the hospital, oblivious to the shenanigans, were delighted with the job and paid up the remainder of the cash. All's well that ends well, and the profit went to pay for some unfortunate's treatment.

Soon other rehabilitation units were copying Nick's work therapy in the hope of raising badly needed income, not realising that a work therapy partnership is very tricky. "I've been told of many units run by desk-jockeys, who think they can organise work-details similar to Chaucer's. Unless the managers have the know-how, come out from their offices, roll up their sleeves and join in, then they will only unleash disasters. I heard of one group from a local alcoholism unit who were left unsupervised to spray paint a wall. They succeeded in spraying most of the directors car, a brand new Audi, bright pink."

Nick admits there have been odd occasions when he was caught out by agreeing, against his better judgement, to become involved with projects over which he has little or no input. There was the case of the curator from a London museum, who had been given a leave of absence to dry out at Chaucer; Nick is always impressed by how such hide-bound institutions take care of their own. Schools, newspapers, law firms, the police, universities will always help out their own drunks, provided the individuals concerned are willing to clean up their act.

In this particular case, the local hospital had recently opened a museum for the hospital estate, and had asked for help cataloguing their displays. Concerned about the member, but needing allies in the hospital, Nick begrudgingly agreed to release the curator on work therapy for a week's trial. After three days he just disappeared, taking valuable items from the hospital collection with him. These items eventually turned up in museums across London, but nobody heard from the curator again.

It takes a great deal of patience, and if necessary Nick will wait for the right set of skills to arrive in the Clinic before embarking on projects. He never forgets that this is work therapy, and the products of the work itself are secondary. Any work is good enough if the therapy is beneficial. "We do get the odd exceptional piece of quality work, but things can also go awry. Then we have to take it on the chin, and either ignore it, or undo the damage and start all over again, but with far more supervision the next time with everyone, from top to bottom of the Clinic, getting involved." It all has to be managed with a good sense of humour. The workers must be treated with respect, not patronised or wrapped in cotton wool. Nick expects them to deliver, but at the same time he watches the members like a hawk. Running these projects with passion, enthusiasm and energy, he never ceases to be amazed at what inspiration, motivation and sheer bloody-mindedness can achieve.

"People will always surprise you, both with good results and bad." At this point in our conversation Nick indicated four garden chairs sitting on his patio. "Notice! One is painted a different colour to the rest. The team ran out of paint, and instead of asking me for more, they did what was obvious to them: they used a different tin that was lying around. The quality of the workmanship was fine - in fact far better than I could do - it was a shame about the colour! When drunks innovate you win some, you lose some."

A Barrel-Load of Monkeys

I then asked Nick whether he had considered using Total Quality Management in the work therapy at the Clinic to improve standards of workmanship. I followed up by introducing Nick to notions like Crosby's 'conformance to requirements,' 'right first time,' and quality circles. Nick started laughing again. "Another one of your lamp-posts, Ian? Another method with which self-delusional bureaucrats pretend they are in control of events. I run work therapy for the therapy not the workmanship. Some of my members are brain damaged; they're just not with it. However, there are others who are only too with it, trying and often succeeding in running rings around me."

Consequently Nick has to watch them like hawks, knowing he is dealing with a barrel-load of monkeys. "They know that I know, and I know that they know that I know! I call it 'drinking thinking.' It explains a lot of their actions during the early days of recovery. For they are still thinking like drunks, and such deception is considered quite normal behaviour. When I think of the number of times they have tried to pull the wool over my eyes over the Clinic's van." One man in particular, John, was always pulling stunts. One relatively quiet weekend, when he thought Nick was out of the way, John hired out the van to an acquaintance, who had promised faithfully to return it by midnight Sunday. The problem is that friends of drunks are often just as unreliable as the drunks themselves. It was mid-morning Monday before the van was delivered back to Chaucer, and the whole scam came to light.

Another weekend John asked if he could borrow the van to move furniture for his sister. The real reason was that a gang of Marauders wanted to sail to France on the ferry in order to fill up with cheap cigarettes and of all things, booze. They all got so drunk on the return journey that they forgot to unload, and that's where Nick found them in the morning, passed out, and the van almost fully loaded with contraband. He had no choice but to kick them all off the programme. "It's sad how drunks can come up with some very imaginative scams, only for the drink to intervene, and they get sloppy at the last hurdle."

There was a story behind that van. It was originally owned by a neighbouring alcoholism unit, which was in direct competition with Chaucer. A senior nurse, Tom Black, usually drove the vehicle. Customised to his specifications, it was both his and his unit's pride and joy. Tom, a real jack-the-lad, used to drop in to Chaucer regularly, on the surface for a social chat with some of the members. In reality he was intent on stealing ideas so that he could use them back at his place.

Over time his van got a little battered, and being very conscious of prestige, Tom wanted to sell the old van and buy a bigger and better one. He started asking around for offers in the region of £5000: no takers. He dropped the price to £3500: still no joy. Then one day a Marauder, who had just returned from visiting a friend in Black's unit, sidled up to Nick and whispered in his ear: "Mr. Black is desperate for £1300 to pay for the new van he has on order."

Drunks are like waiters: nobody sees them. The most sensitive details are discussed in front of them as if they aren't there, or are too stupid to understand what's going on. Nick has often used the tactic of playing the ex-drunk himself, to great advantage: "It always pays to get an opponent to underestimate you." There being a history of confrontation between himself and Black, Nick couldn't just ask him directly if he would consider an offer in the region of £1300, as that would certainly raise his suspicions. So on Black's next visit to Chaucer, just as Teresa escorted him into the office, a forewarned Nick stood inside with his back to the door, apparently unaware of his visitor, talking loudly to the dialling tone of the phone: "I can only offer you £1350 for your van. I'm sorry but I just can't afford your price." And so it was Chaucer bought its first van for a knockdown price.

That van was jinxed from the start. It caused Nick no end of trouble. He once sent two members to a local garage to pick up parts for a roof rack, which they were to fit to the van. They took most of the day over the job, and when they had finished they parked it, and surreptitiously left the keys at reception. Nick thought they had slid off a little too quickly, so he checked. They hadn't used any washers when bolting the rack down, and furthermore one bolt was missing. They had spent some of the money he had given them on cigarettes; there was only enough cash to buy the nuts and bolts, but not the washers. However, that didn't explain the missing bolt. It turned out the garage only had eleven bolts in stock, so they gave the drunks one short of the full order; after all everyone would think the drunks had done a bad job or had lost the twelfth bolt.

"They're sober drunks; not yet mentally lucid, they're devious, they're amoral and have no sense of shame." When Nick confronted them they proudly told him exactly what had happened! Nick knows the way drunks think, and so he under-stood their actions. He'd been there, done that. So he couldn't blame them. But what was the garage's excuse of cheating them? They didn't need an excuse! The inescapable fact is that every-body's at it, not just drunks.

"So Ian, come off that high-minded total quality nonsense. Every employee in every company will pull a stunt like this, on their customers or their employers, if it gets them out of a jam and they think they can get away with it. They may even do it just to relieve the boredom. Everyone has lateral loyalties and hidden agendas.

Let's not pretend. When circumstances conspire then everyone will get up to no good. That is why I always start out with suspicion. My trust has to be earned over time." How strange! Nick seemed to be coming to the conclusion that drunks are no different to everyone else; but at least the drunks can blame their amorality and duplicity on the booze.

All Property is Theft

The booze taught Nick to be devious, so he's not surprised when members pull a few scams from time to time. One of the cheekiest concerned four hospital-owned bungalows situated nearby. They were used as accommodation for staff from the old Chaucer ward. However the staff moved out about a month after the ward was closed down, and the bungalows were abandoned along with the Chaucer ward. The hospital planned to sell that part of the site, including the Chaucer building, for housing development once they had received a good offer and of course after planning permission had been granted. As far as they were concerned, the bungalows weren't rented accommodation but a demolition job in waiting.

This opportunity proved too good to miss for John and some of his capitalist mates among the Marauders. They tidied up all four buildings and John pinned a note on the notice board outside the staff canteen of the main hospital, announcing that he had bungalows to let. The note gave a phone number on which interested parties could contact one Nicholas Charles of Chaucer Clinic after seven o'clock in the evening. The reason for the late hour was so that Mr. Charles could show anyone interested immediately around the accommodation. The telephone involved was situated in a public call box in the Chaucer Reception area. John haunted that phone box for the next two evenings taking all in-coming calls. After seven o'clock the real Nick was long gone home, and so the coast was clear for his masquerade.

It only took two days for John to find tenants, and the incriminating notice was quickly removed. Then four different families moved in, agreeing that John a.k.a. 'Nicholas Charles' would personally call around each week to collect the rent in cash. Month followed uneventful month until the fateful day when a problem cropped up with the plumbing in one of the bungalows. Naturally the occupant went straight up to Chaucer to seek help.

As fate would have it, the first person they met at Chaucer Reception was the real Nick Charles. They asked for Mr. Charles, and he, naturally, replied: "yes, I'm Nick Charles, can I help you?"

"But you aren't Nicholas Charles!" and the whole tangled web unfolded. It turned out that John - not nearly as daft as everybody thought - had spotted in the hospital system an example of the general confusion that pervades every large bureaucratic institution. All he had to do was work out how to take advantage of the chaos. And take advantage he did. That was how employees of the Health Authority came to pay rent to a drunk in order to stay in buildings that were owned by the said Health Authority, but which they had forgotten about.

Ice Cream Men

Chaucer has had more than its fair share of capitalists among the Marauders. A 'Mr. Whippy-type' ice-cream van had been abandoned on the hospital estate. It had been involved in a local turf war. An opposing gang of ice-cream vendors had stolen it, drained it of oil, and then ran the engine until it seized up.

A gleeful band of Marauders came across it and pushed it back to the Clinic building. Disappointed that the engine was useless, they were overjoyed to discover that the ice cream maker was still in working order. They talked of making millions, and the prospect of a magnificent new clinic building appeared before their eyes! A relatively small financial outlay produced 18 gallons of ice cream.

All they needed now were customers. It was October and raining. They started by intercepting visitors to nearby St Bernard's Hospital, but were soon moved on by the hospital authorities. They ended up on a side road, about 200 yards from the Clinic, but with no passing trade. Now parked opposite a derelict building, there was no prospect of finding customers.

Then something very mysterious happened. The abandoned building caught fire! Four fire brigade appliances rushed to the scene to put out the blaze, and the ice cream was sold out in less than an hour to the firemen and to the crowd of onlookers who had gathered to watch the blaze.

Fine Art

One of Chaucer's members was 'McGillicuddy,' a world-famous counterfeiter of masterpieces. He had been jailed for his part in a major scandal that involved selling his paintings as originals by Picasso and Degas. He was out on bail, attending Chaucer for rehabilitation from alcohol addiction. Part of his bail conditions was that he should not earn any money from his painting. That's exactly what McGillicuddy did, to the letter. He went around the hospital and the local vicinity offering to paint people for free, however, he insisted that he was paid to 'go away,' but only after the portrait was completed. Such was his fame that he had a waiting list!

Aerial, the Black Cat

Chaucer's black tomcat was known to everyone as Aerial. Quite a reasonable name since he slept on the third floor roof, draped precariously around the television aerial. Then the fateful day arrived when, thanks to a generous donation from Barings Bank, a new kitchen was to be built. The general refurbishment meant that the aerial had to be moved a distance of some 200 feet away from the cat's favourite resting place. Nick was told that the cheapest estimate for the removal and relocation was £180.

Refitting the aerial in its new location was going to be easy, but getting it down from its present position was a rather tricky job. One of our heroes stepped into the breach. "I'll do it for £50." He and Nick shook hands on the deal. The following day a crowd began to gather around the Marauder. He was running around excitedly, shouting and screaming, pointing up at the cat, which, as usual, was fast asleep with just the aerial for support, some 60 feet above the ground. "Call the fire brigade," an anonymous voice shouted. The brave fire-fighters duly arrived to rescue the cat. Our marauder sidled up to the leading fireman. "It's worth £25 to bring the aerial down while you're up there." Job done.

10

Chaucer is Dead.
Long live Chaucer!

Even as they moved into the old Chaucer Ward and started
clearing up the mess, Nick knew that the axe would eventually
fall on their occupancy. However, by then he had already burnt all
his bridges. Chaucer was taking one hundred and ten percent of
his time, and so he had wound down all his extra-curricular activities. Then in September 1990, the news finally came through that
they had one year to find new accommodation. The hospital had
found a buyer who wanted to bulldoze the area composed of the
old Chaucer Ward along with the other numerous T-wards, the
bungalows, and a whole lot more. The development company
were intent on growing the ultimate cash crop: houses. The clock
had started ticking; Chaucer would have to go.

But go where? Onto the stage strode two more heroes: Abdy
Richardson, the Chairman of the Hospital Trust, and Eddie Kane,
the Chief Executive. Both had been very supportive of Nick
during his tenure at the hospital because they recognised the
valuable services that Chaucer was providing for the general
health care of the local community, and they admired the way
Nick 'got things done.' Despite much opposition, and there was
quite a bit within the hospital from for example the Max Glatt
ward (the statutory rehab ward in the hospital), these two most
senior hospital officials were keen for Chaucer's work to continue.
Consequently, the pair set about finding an alternative site for the
Clinic. They showed Nick around a wide range of possibilities.
However, only one building held any interest for him, and that
was Linden House, a ward of the old Hanwell Asylum just a few
hundred yards from the present Chaucer. It had been a geriatric
home, but it had been badly damaged by a fire, and so the
patients had moved out.

Fire was an ever-present problem in all the buildings on this neglected far-flung western arm of the hospital empire. Situated a long way from the main building, and not on any main thoroughfare, gradually over the years it had become littered with derelict buildings and abandoned machinery. Garbage was blowing around everywhere. As time went by the problems only got worse. The area was the haunting ground for all the local ne'er-do-wells and down-and-outs who, to keep warm and to cook, would light fires anywhere and everywhere. Where there's a dosser, there's a fire.

The local low-class prostitutes also moved into some of the abandoned wards, plying their trade on the discarded hospital beds that had been unspeakably soiled over the intervening months. It was not unusual for potential clients of one particular 'lady of the night' to knock on Chaucer's door asking for directions to 'Sandra's place.'

Nick decided that, with a little muscle power from the Marauders, he would clean up the whole area, so intent was he on getting Linden House to replace Chaucer. He promised the hospital authorities that, if he were finally allowed into Linden House, he would evict both the tarts and the dossers. As usual the hospital's left hand didn't know what the right was doing. A group of Queen Charlotte's Nurses had also been given permission by another administrative department to move into the ground floor of Linden House, which, unlike the rest of the building, was just about habitable. The nurses, however, were horrified to discover that their unwanted neighbours, the dossers, would climb into the upper floor rooms every evening. As if it wasn't bad enough that these degenerates would break into the nurses' accommodation to steal money and property, they also had a habit of lighting their fires on the bare floorboards above the nurses' sleeping quarters.

The Ghosts of Linden House

Consequently, Nick was confident that the Queen Charlotte nurses, in fear of their lives, would eventually move out. He had Eddie Kane's verbal agreement that he could move in, provided the hospital didn't decide to sell the property. So Nick organised the workers from Chaucer to start redecorating Linden House from late November in preparation for the move sometime the following autumn.

Always at the back of his mind, however, was a worry that the company already developing part of the site would expand their land grab, and bid to add Linden House to their portfolio of properties. Something had to be done!

Michael, the boss of an interested developer, was very superstitious: not really surprising since a few months earlier, a few days after having walked under a ladder, he'd been badly injured in a serious car smash. In fact he was so superstitious that he used to visit a psychic twice a week to have his fortune told; he wanted to be forewarned of any future accidents. Nick saw an opportunity in this, and so he set about hatching a devious plot: Linden House was to have its own resident ghost! Then Michael and his builders were sure to steer well clear of the place.

Whenever the Marauders were renovating Linden House they would always leave a night watchman on guard so that the dossers wouldn't steal their tools and equipment. One particular night, when Sean O'Farrell, a trusted Chaucer employee and founder member, had drawn the short straw for guarding Linden House, Nick decided to strike. He would come into the building late at night, turn the lights on and off, bang doors, moan and groan, and generally haunt the place. Sean was forewarned of what Nick had in mind so as not to panic him.

Nick had to go through the whole charade because he couldn't rely on Sean inventing a convincing account of the haunting all by himself. Then, on the following morning, Sean could honestly recount a long tale of things that went bump in the night, without embellishments, and thereby start and spread the rumour of the Ghost of Linden House. If Nick could keep this up for a week, he'd be sure to frighten everyone away, especially Michael.

It was a great idea, but unfortunately Nick was dining out at a local restaurant with Kelly, Nikki and Teresa that evening, and the plan completely slipped his mind. The next morning, a shame-faced Nick went to apologise to Sean, when he was met with: "Dat was f******g brilliant las' night. How'd y'do dat? Dat f******g woman cummin' through dat f******g wall. 'Er mop 'at, an' ol' fashioned starchy nurse's outfit. Did yer get it from d'Joke Shop. All that bangin' an' crashin.' She went straight through d'wall, and f*****g came back again. How'd y'do dat? Bloody brilliant."

An embarrassed Nick explained that he had completely forgotten about the plan. "Stop windin' me up. I chatted to 'er for Gordsake! Twice I asked you t'make us a f*****g cuppa ... but you f*****g didn't answer!" The profanities suddenly stopped as the enormity of Nick's words struck home. As a drunk, Sean had got used to hallucinating. Even now, recently reformed, he was still living on the cusp of reality. The weirdness of events from the previous night, including the physical impossibility of passing through walls, just hadn't occurred to him. However, in the pale light of day, the realisation of his close encounter soon had Sean hyper-ventilating. From that moment on, Sean refused to go anywhere near the top floor of Linden House unless he was accompanied by at least two others.

The word spread like wildfire: Linden House was haunted. However, not everyone was as chicken as Sean; Nick was swamped with volunteers who wanted to spend the night there. The ghost was seen a few times over the next couple of weeks, but then it all went very quiet. It was a whole ten months before she was spotted again, by of all people, John Mahoney, a killer and all-round hard-man. Mahoney is afraid of no man. He is, however, terrified of two women. From the moment she interviewed him on his entry to Chaucer, he was "scared s***less of Nikki," and now a second lady doubled his fearful list: a small spectral matron decked out in a mop hat and nineteenth century nurse's uniform. As for Nick, he never did witness the apparition, however, that didn't stop him saying that he had spotted it regularly in those intervening ten months - after all he had to keep up the pretence. It worked! Paddy and the developers lost interest, and Linden House was finally Nick's.

The phantom still appears from time to time, causing terror and consternation among Chaucer's members. More recently, however, Linden House has been honoured with the appearance of a second ghost, but this time a much more welcome apparition. The ghost of Big Ron, the Clinic's cat, who died in 1999 after a long and contented life at Chaucer, still pads the corridors. Big Ron, an overweight black and white feline named after 'Big Ron' Saunders the erstwhile manager of Aston Villa Football Club (what else!), keeps the phantom nurse company and purrs at anyone willing to listen, especially Nikki, his lifelong friend.

All Quiet on the Western Front

The Queen Charlotte Nurses were still waiting to be re-housed when, one very cold night just before Christmas 1990, some dossers broke into the upper floors of Linden House. The fire they lit to keep themselves warm took hold of the floorboards, then the walls, and ceilings. Soon the whole central section of the house was ablaze. What the fire didn't destroy, the fire brigade finished off with their hoses. The nurses moved out, and once again the building, one part badly charred and the remainder smoke- and water-damaged, was finally available.

Nick went straight over to Eddie and told him that, despite the fire damage, he still wanted Linden House. Eddie knew of the mess in the building, and this time there weren't just huge holes in the roof - there was no roof. Eddie was amazed that Nick was still keen to move in, and he readily gave his permission, knowing this time there would be no more resistance from his colleagues among the hospital administrators. This latest conflagration had brought the hospital management to its wit's end about what to do with the problem of the dossers and their fire-raising antics in the thirty-plus abandoned buildings at the western end of the estate. They called it the 'Wild West;' the local fire brigade had a season ticket to the site, as every week throughout the winter a fire would break out somewhere in the T-wards. These wards had all been damaged to various degrees of severity at some time or other over the past year.

But despite the extensive damage, Nick still retained his dream of what Linden House could become. His offer to police the western outpost of the estate in return for occupancy of Linden House was the answer to the hospital management's prayers. However, no date was fixed for the move. Nick had a year's notice on Chaucer Ward and didn't have to be out until September 1991. However, he wasn't going to hang around. From Christmas 1990 he surreptitiously started moving into Linden House, repairing, refurbishing and generally tidying up. The unwritten promise of Eddie Kane and Abdy Richardson was good enough for him.

An Exit of Choice

Nick immediately reconfirmed his pact to tame the wild frontier. The hospital security men only ever ventured this far westward twice a day: around 6pm to lock the West Gate, the underused access to the site, and again around 7am to re-open it. That may have stopped cars coming onto the site, but dossers don't have cars, and the down-and-outs have little difficulty in climbing over an unguarded gate even though it is fifteen feet high.

It wasn't only the dossers who climbed the gate. Being only a few yards from Chaucer, it was the exit of choice for Clinic members too. The local tobacconist was just a few minutes away through (or over) the gate, whereas the alternative routes involved a walk of at least a mile. To aid their escape some members had used a car-jack to force apart the bars of the gate. However, some members like Frank, who were a little too broad around the beam to squeeze through, still had to climb the gate to collect their 'fags.' Frank, the Clinic's 'spiv,' and a notorious womaniser, always came and went this way. Returning from a date one evening, he was on his way back to the Clinic for supper when he met up with an old acquaintance who had just robbed a local clothes shop, a not unusual occurrence. Frank bought four pairs of Levis and a flashy pair of cowboy boots. A snappy dresser, he couldn't wait so he changed into his new gear behind a wall, keeping three pairs of jeans back to sell in the Clinic. He wanted to make a big impression when he made his entrance at supper.

Outside the West Gate, Frank pushed the stolen Levis through the gap and started to climb over. Suddenly a dosser appeared from nowhere on the other side of the gate. He grabbed the three pairs of jeans, and 'legged it.' Shouting and screaming Frank rushed his ascent, intending to chase the thief. However, he was a little shaky on his legs, although this time due to this exertions, and not the booze. His afternoon of passion had tired him out. Worse, the soles of his new boots were very shiny too. Frank slipped, and one of his new boots became tangled on the spikes. He fell backwards tearing that boot, and breaking his left leg in the process. Frank crashed fifteen feet to the ground, landing heavily on his right leg, which was also fractured.

He lay there, moaning in pain. The few pedestrians who passed by, taking him for a drunk, gave him a wide berth. A few members inside the gate also saw him lying on the ground, but they assumed that Frank, a regular joker, was just messing around. Only one Good Samaritan, a very pregnant woman, came to his aid. She rushed across the road to a nearby telephone box and called for an ambulance. However, the excitement was all too much for her, and she started to go into labour. The ambulance duly arrived, but it took her off to hospital, leaving poor Frank still lying unseen across the road outside the West Gate.

He was there for over an hour, when John Grey, who had popped out for a smoke during supper, spotted Frank through the gate. "I've broken me bloody legs, get me a f*****g ambulance." The immediate response from John was: "So you won't be 'aving your dinner then? Can I 'ave it." These words may seem callous to any sober citizen, but in the self-centred survivalist logic of a drunk (even recently sober), it was an obvious and perfectly understandable request. Drunks don't have the luxury of compassion. They must operate within a pitiless capitalist ethic just to survive. Even in the ordinary day-to-day running of Chaucer, the drunks have established a secondary market where members swap their meals for cigarettes.

Frank certainly understood the situation, for even with his two broken legs he wanted to know "what'll you gimme for it." After much bartering, the final price of two bandages from the First Aid Box in Chaucer was handed over. Then in a weak voice, he asked John about when the ambulance was coming.

"Amblance? I din't call no amblance! I jus' brought the bandages, and I'm off to 'ave your supper. Jus' jokin'!" Two very long and pain-filled hours after his fall, the ambulance finally arrived. John set off to have Frank's dinner, but he was stopped in his tracks by the most terrifying screams, and looked back. "It was jus' like in *Psycho*." He ran back to the Gate expecting to see Frank in agony, having his bones reset. Not so. The ambulance men hadn't got that far. Frank was in hysterics as they tried to cut off his brand new jeans to check on his injuries. Poor Frank! One pair of jeans ruined, three stolen, and his left cowboy boot torn beyond repair. His right boot was as good as new though, and Nikki now keeps that in her office as a trophy - waiting for a one-legged cowboy maybe?

As for the ambulance, instead of taking Frank to Ealing hospital, less than half a mile away, it drove instead the five congested miles to Hammersmith. Their action does beg the question of

whether Frank and John's behaviour is any weirder than that of
the paramedics, or the hospital system for that matter!

Moving House

Slowly and surely the Wild West was tamed as the destructive
(and self-destructive) homeless dossers were eased out. Nick and
Teresa can still remember the happy day when the very last of
these troublesome vagrants, who refused offers of treatment, was
finally moved on. But that was still months away in the future.
First, there was still the matter of the huge amount of work
needed to repair the fire and water damage in Linden House, just
to make it habitable.

Nick had no problem in finding the labour for the work; he had all
the free manpower he could possibly need from among the
Chaucer members. However, the building material was another
matter altogether. Nick's solution was obvious, and lying all
around him. He would set the Marauders to scavenging. They
scoured the site. Every abandoned T-ward, every out-building,
even Old Chaucer Ward, which was also soon to be demolished,
were stripped. Nothing was overlooked: roof-slates, rafters, floorboards, bricks, window frames, glass; you name it, they took it.
They even rescued (!) the substantial old-fashioned wooden doors
and doorframes from old Chaucer; after nailing chipboard over
the doorways no one was any the wiser.

Month after month, the systematic scavenging continued.
Anything and everything useful was collected, and stored safe
from prying eyes and thieving hands. For when the word finally
got out that a large swathe of the hospital site was being redevel-
oped, it seemed that the whole of Britain got to hear about it.
Every 'rag-and-bone man' in the country wanted his share of the
rich pickings. A gang of 'gypos' even sailed down from the
Midlands along the Grand Union Canal; they had heard there was
lead to be 'nicked.' They knocked a hole in the boundary wall
between the hospital and the canal, ready to make their getaway
by sailing off with the spoils. Their timing couldn't have been
worse. All they found were poor Sean O'Farrell and Micky
Meeson doing a final check of the grounds; the Marauders had left
nothing. The 'gypos,' furious to find that the cupboard was bare,
set about putting Sean and Micky in hospital with broken ribs and
various lacerations.

Although Chaucer's notice to quit didn't expire until September 1991, and still with no officially sanctioned moving day, by April Nick had already had enough of waiting. He went to Eddie Kane's office and told the Chief Executive that he intended to move as soon as possible. Kane agreed: they could have Linden House, but not it's annexe; the hospital were considering other possibilities for that. "So you agree we can have Linden House. That's just as well, because we're moving in there as we speak," was Nick's parting shot as he left a smiling Eddie's office.

On that day, April 15th 1991, the members of Chaucer packed up their possessions, placed them on their beds, and trundled en masse down the road. Luckily, their beds were on wheels! Although it would be months before all the smoke damage was finally cleared, the new Clinic was already up and running. However, not everyone was happy with the move. Nikki, who by now was well on the way to becoming an important member of the team, and who merited her own office, had a lot of blood sweat and tears invested in Chaucer Mark One. Convinced they would be moving back, she refused to move.

Nick told himself that Nikki would eventually turn up at Linden House, tail between her legs. Two hours went by, and still no Nikki. A very concerned Nick returned to Chaucer One and found her staring blankly out of her office window at the 40-foot fir tree outside. That view was important to her; she had earned that view. Nick, as only Nick can, came up with a typical Nick solution. He told Nikki that as part of their transfer to Chaucer Two they were going to transplant the big fir tree. A surprised Nikki grudgingly moved out. A man of his word, Nick organised a gang of Marauders, not the most professional of arboriculturists, to move the fir: quite an undertaking. Not unexpectedly, the poor tree slowly died over the next few months, but by then Nikki had happily settled in at Linden House, and she said no more about it.

Should Nick call the new Clinic 'Linden House?' No! By now the drunks and the authorities across the land knew of Chaucer; so that name would stay. Chaucer Mark One was dead (almost); long live Chaucer Mark Two! Almost dead? From the April to the official end of the notice to quit old Chaucer in the September, Nick was running two clinics simultaneously. He did this because he couldn't officially move in to Linden House until the new clinic

had been licensed, and to be licensed the building had to be
inspected. That was a problem. There was no way Linden House
would pass an inspection; it didn't even have a complete roof!

Another Chaucer, Another Roof!

What is it about Chaucer and roofs? This was the third time that a
Chaucer roof had to be fixed. On the two previous occasions Pete
Townshend had come to the rescue. However, this time Nick
didn't need to ask for the musician's support. The Marauders had
scavenged sufficient material from all the other abandoned wards;
they'd even exchanged some of the old-fashioned heavy wood
doors for large quantities of paint. Unfortunately it was all going
to take quite a time. The problem was that Nick needed an inspection as soon as possible, in order to get the licence that would
allow him to run the Clinic. They could do a passable redecoration
job on the ward quite quickly, but the roof was another matter
altogether; they just didn't have the time.

Yet again, necessity was the mother of invention. Nick had read in
the local newspaper that the Boy Scouts in the area had recently
replaced their old-fashioned greased-tarpaulin tents with sexy
new brightly coloured ones made from the latest man-made
fibres. He contacted the scout leader immediately and offered to
buy six of their old tents. By a sheer fluke, the old tarpaulins were
just the right dimensions for the roof. Nick, together with Sean
O'Farrell, who was now confident that the ghostly nurse had been
smoked out of her haunting habits, set about erecting all six tents
in the attic, finishing the job off by nailing the tent-flaps to the
walls.

The building was now waterproof, but a canvas roof certainly
wouldn't pass an official inspection. Hence the final act of genius.
They would fasten roof-slates to the fabric with wood glue.
Behold! It looked like a roof at a distance, but not close up. That
didn't matter because the inspectors would only see it from
ground level and from about 100 yards away: even that view was
at an oblique angle. Although it took only a few hours to
construct, the temporary pre'fabric'ated roof served its purpose.
Chaucer Mark Two passed its inspection and opened for business.
It was over fourteen months before they found time to replace the
canvas canopy with a proper slate roof from materials scavenged
from the old wards.

Things were going well, until one evening in 1994 when they were forced to evacuate the building as smoke started pouring through the barrier that separated Linden House from its annexe. Some dossers had returned temporarily, and finding the annexe unoccupied, accidentally set fire to the place. Thankfully, every cloud (of smoke) has a silver lining. The hospital authorities, exasperated by yet another fire, told Nick he could do them a favour by annexing the annexe. This is how Chaucer came to be the shape it is, some ten times the original size of Chaucer Mark One.

Always look a Gift Horse in the Mouth

They had moved in, but as usual there was an acute shortage of money. In fact there were bad times when the money was so tight that Nick, Kelly, Nikki and Teresa couldn't take a penny in salary for their work; there was just nothing in the bank. However, Chaucer's troubles seemed to be over when they were approached by a 'friend,' Sharon, who offered to donate a large sum to the Clinic in return for a job and somewhere to live; a request that was easily supplied within the new Chaucer infrastructure. It seemed like an answer to their prayers. Today, an older and wiser Nick would have turned such an offer down flat, seeing TROUBLE written all over it.

However, back then they accepted. An emotionally unstable Sharon had just separated from her husband, and the money was part of the financial settlement of her divorce. Within weeks her deal with Nick went sour. A new lover, Wayne, had turned up on the scene, no doubt attracted by the cash, but totally unaware that the money had been donated to the Clinic. He was intent on getting the money back, and set about poisoning Sharon's mind against Chaucer.

Wayne's demands for the return of the money were accompanied by his persistent stalking and intimidation of Nick and his colleagues. The pair was caught by the police attempting to interfere with the brakes on Nick's car at 3am one morning, and they even cut his TV/Satellite cable connection in the dead of night. Worse, Nick's cat, Marriott, was stabbed and needed many stitches; thankfully he recovered fully and lived on contentedly for a further dozen years. The campaign against Nick and Chaucer was relentless, and the whole saga dragged on for several years. Nick eventually decided to cut his losses and returned the money, however the legal complications with the Charity Commission of reversing such a donation into a personal loan to Nick ended up costing him a great deal of money.

Wayne wasn't very bright, and he had no idea that he was a rank amateur in the intimidation stakes. Chaucer, on the other hand, was full of professionals. Nick has saved many of those professionals (intimidators that is), including convicted murderers and violent criminals, from their addiction, and they are loyal to a fault. There is nothing they wouldn't do for him: absolutely nothing. Despite the presence of these 'heavies,' in some ways Chaucer is a fairly easy-going place; members wander freely around everywhere. Consequently if someone is causing trouble for Nick, pretty soon the whole Clinic gets to know about it. And that's when the problems arise. Some members see themselves as heroes coming to Nick's rescue, whether he asks for it or not.

Wayne's on-going campaign of hate against Nick couldn't be kept a secret for long, and the attack on Marriott was the last straw for two particularly soft-centred 'hard-men' in the Clinic. They would 'sort it.' With all their contacts in the criminal fraternity, it wasn't difficult for them to obtain a sawn-off shotgun and cartridges. They found Wayne's address, and set off to lie in wait.

Of course this pair were not the subtlest of hit-men. They had told anyone in the Clinic who would listen what they had planned. Word eventually got back to a horrified Nick, who immediately jumped in his car and rushed out to 'head them off at the pass.' He spotted the two villains loitering outside Wayne's house, and shouted: "You stupid b******s, get into this f******g car right now." Shamefaced, the two assassins plus the shot-gun shambled into Nick's car, just as Wayne, dressed in track-suit and trainers, left the house - oblivious to the fact that had he started his jog a minute earlier he would now be dead meat. Nick drove straight to the river, tossed the gun in the Thames, and all three returned to Chaucer in silence.

A Perverted Loyalty?
If only the ambush had been an isolated incident! Thankfully the vast majority of Chaucer's members are not criminals, rather they are drawn from across the whole of British society; the only common factor is an addiction to drink. However, to say that

some of the alcoholics admitted to Chaucer have been 'dangerous' from time to time would be a gross understatement, several of them with so-called 'respectable' upbringing.

Nick is convinced that much of the aggression he and Nikki confront in their initial interviews with potential clients, and not just with the criminals, is that the interviewees are drunks who still don't know, or won't admit, that they are drunks. When members sign up for Chaucer that residual aggression is often sublimated, but it can explode into the open at any time. On one occasion a call came through on the public phone for a member who had skipped off for the day. The usual procedure was for someone to take a message and pin it up on the notice board - but not this one: "The hit's off because the ammunition hasn't come!" The member in question never returned to Chaucer, and the message remained undelivered.

So how does Nick keep this strange assortment of staff and members under some semblance of control? "It's not from reading books about Human Resource Management!" When I talked to Nick about all the latest theories, particularly about 'Empowerment,' the response was immediate and straight to the point: "Empowerment my a**e; power isn't given, power is taken. The only way to empower employees is to trust them." Not surprising then that in 'management speak' the word empower-ment is usually preferred to trust, particularly among hypocritical and psychopathic managers who scream and shout at their employees, and then wonder why their company is going downhill. Cowed employees never take risks, and without risk there can be no success; risk-taking is after all the whole idea behind empowerment.

There is so much nonsense talked about trust and loyalty in management. Trust, and mutual loyalty, both involve taking risks with people. Nick himself has numerous stories about misplaced loyalty, both towards him (like with our the two hit-men) and by him, but that has been more than compensated by successful relationships. His approach, grounded in trust, is at the very base of Nick's attitude towards staff management, and of his handling of members. This is obvious from his bond with the Marauders, and theirs with him. That trust must be mutual, but not blind. In the early stages of a relationship trust must be given, but with reservations. Trust must be tested so that it can be earned. Then trust accumulates, however, if for any reason that trust is deliberately abused, then there is no way back.

As far as Nick is concerned, making mistakes, as long as they are genuine, is just part of the learning curve, and a way of discovering ones limitations. He expects people to operate within their limits, but he always keeps testing and stretching those limits. Nick is aware that in his blatantly optimistic approach towards people who have been rejected by society, and in his belief of their potential, he is taking enormous risks. When he talks about it dispassionately, away from the pressures of Chaucer, his attitude may even appear nonsensical. However, the moment he starts recounting his stories, in the immediacy of the context of Chaucer Clinic, it all makes perfect sense.

Good Enough?

Nick is quite clear: mollycoddling is not the answer. Mutual respect means forcing (often unreasonable) expectations on staff and members. There is always an element of both 'carrot and stick' in his management style. However there can be no hard and fast set of rules; "circumstances alter cases," as Nick is so fond of saying. A new staff regime was introduced, which meant the staff had to send text messages on mobile phones instead of internal memos. One man couldn't grasp the technique, so he was locked in the toilet with a book of instructions and told he could only come out when Nick received a text message asking for him to be released.

One trainee member of staff had a chronic stutter/speech impediment caused by alcohol. Nick put him on the reception desk: a task that involved answering incoming calls on the switchboard. His problem was eventually solved, but only after one of the longest telephone assessments on record.

It took a whole day's 'training' to convince the newly promoted head of the gardening department that two tins of 2-stroke oil did not equal the one tin of 4-stroke required by the lawn mower.

A trainee chef (a former 'member') was told to stop giving people different amounts of food based on whom he liked and disliked. He was told he must treat everyone exactly the same. There must be no exceptions. The chef asked Nick what he should do about the member who always ate one mouthful and then threw the rest away - to which Nick replied, "give him the same meat and three veg., but make each portion smaller." That's Nick Charles's logic!

Nick admitted an alcoholic to the Clinic, who was also an anorexic. It was not the first time. At dinnertime she was made to sit down and eat with the group, but unlike the other diners she was given a large plate with a shaving of carrot, half a sprout, a pea and half a tiny, tiny new potato, and finally, a quarter inch square of meat. Everyone else sat down alongside and demolished a normal sized meal. Nothing whatsoever was said, not even when half a prune with the faintest yellow stains of custard arrived. In no time at all the now ex-anorexic was eating normal portions without question.

Nick had already treated Nikki de Villiers for alcoholism and anorexia in this way, and with such success that he had no hesitation in using the same method on others. While he sees alcoholism as a disease, Nick reluctantly admits that he is less inclined to view anorexia with the same sympathy. He is the first to admit "I am not an authority on anorexia, having treated only six in my career, all of them alongside alcoholism. However, my no-nonsense alcohol treatment, rooted in re-education and re-integration, seems to work with anorexics. I have a 100% record thus far. So why should I change to someone else's methods? Admittedly not all go on to be gluttons, but they regularly eat balanced meals."

This is just another example of how Nick Charles's outrageous approaches can often prove effective. However, Nick insists that he would never recommend this heavy-handed method as a general cure for anorexia. He only uses it alongside specific guidance and training in all facets of its application, but he stands by the method unequivocally. And "I do have ex-anorexic Nikki keeping a very close eye on things."

A live-in employee showed an element of defiance by refusing to answer the telephone after 6pm. Her punishment was to man the all night help-line for the next six weeks. Thereafter she was always first to the phone, anytime, anywhere. A paternal Nick treats everyone in the Clinic like a member of his family; they may have their squabbles, but in the end they always make up. That's how Chaucer works; it just wouldn't function if it were run as a business.

Peter de Villiers, who runs the guided tours for visitors to the Clinic, is one of the real characters on the Chaucer staff. He took his last drink at 1.30pm July 1992. Peter is Nikki's ex-husband; they were married and divorced when they were both still drunks. Now they are very good friends, although Nikki is the boss. Peter, a charmer and a natural in public relations, was chosen to be the first Tour Guide for Chaucer. On his first day he listened to Nikki's directions very carefully, taking in every word and offering his own suggestions from time to time. After several dummy runs he was finally ready for his first major conducted tour, that of six social workers from East London. The group met up in reception, and Peter introduced himself with a brief resume of his life and times. He then turned around and set off, happily chatting about different aspects of the Clinic. Several minutes later he was approached by an irate Nikki, who asked him sarcastically how the tour was going. "Excellent," he said, without hesitation. "Then why are all our guests still standing in reception?"

Chaucer's IT expert Chris is a recovered alcoholic, who has suffered severe neurological damage. This has seriously affected his balance, to the point where he keeps falling over - a very common ailment among alcoholics, sober or drunk. On several occasions, as Nick was attempting to hold a conversation with him, he would topple over and disappear behind his desk. Nick was concerned that he might suffer an accident while working alone, so he was provided with a mobile phone. On the very first night he was urinating in the lavatory, when he fell and the new phone went straight down the pan, and was a write-off. Without batting an eyelid, Nick gave Chris a new phone and told him "it's alright, I can't p*** and talk at the same time either."

In an effort to maintain a happy workplace, Nick insists that everyone adopts a happy smile. He has set a fine of £1 for anyone caught not smiling. He even asks that they try to turn any bad news into good. All went well until a trainee member of staff assured a young widow that the death of her elderly alcoholic husband had given her the opportunity to marry someone of her own age. He delivered this news with the obligatory huge smile on his face, while the widow broke down and sobbed hysterically. Subsequently, the staff at Chaucer is more circumspect about smiling arbitrarily. Nick calculates that at the last count he is owed around £50,000 in fines. He is also much more careful about taking recovered alcoholics onto the staff too soon.

Nick was showing Miriam, a new secretary, how to transcribe his tape-recorded words into a word processor. He asked her if she had completed a recently dictated six pages of corrections. "Yes," she said, "near enough."
"Near enough's not good enough. Go back and do it again - I want it spot on," Nick replied.
When Miriam returned, he asked the same question. "It really is near enough this time," she said.
"Take it away and don't come back until it's spot on," he thundered.
Half an hour later she returned again and excitedly announced. "It's spot on this time, boss."
"Good," he said. "That's near enough!"

'Stories? I've got thousands of them!" I often wonder what a typical Human Resources Manager would do in Nick's place; then again perhaps I'd rather not know. Chaucer members come from all social strata, from all races and religions. They are of both sexes, and of all shapes, sizes and sexual proclivities. There have been anonymous, insignificant, and ignored members of society: real Mr Cellophanes. There have also been brutal criminals and murderers, like three-time killer John Mahoney - a terrifying sight, with a body totally covered in tattoos, and that includes his shaven head. However, as newly dried-out drunks, there is one thing they all have in common: any residue of personal pride or social decency has been burned away by alcohol. You would think that keeping some semblance of control over this motley crew would be Nick's biggest headache. Think again! Dealing with drunks, both members and the caring staff of Chaucer (who are all ex-drunks) is child's play when compared with the idiotic bureaucrats (thankfully only a small minority) whose job it is to waste as much of Nick's patience, time, money and energy as they can: as we shall see in the next chapter.

11

Battling with Bureaucracy

"So what do you make of Chaucer, Ian?" Teresa was keen to know my impression after my first of many visits researching this book. My reaction, after spending the day talking with her, with Nick, Nikki, the rest of the staff, and some of the members, surprised her. I hadn't known what to expect: possibly a stressful and depressing 'institution.' What I found was a pleasant, up-beat and cheerful atmosphere, and a positive 'can do' attitude in everyone.

However, what hit me most forcibly not only that first time, but also on all subsequent visits, was that their biggest headache wasn't dealing with disruptive and possibly violent drunks, but rather the sheer nonsense that the Chaucer staff regularly suffers from petty officialdom - a stupidity they have endured from the Clinic's very first days. That stupidity is getting worse, with a flurry of new regulations, all adding to the costs of the Clinic - all reinforcing my day-one realisation that Chaucer was a black hole for Nick's money.

Pensions-in-Waiting

The only time any sign of gloom and anger crept into our conversations was when this question of bureaucracy raised its nonsensical head. Teresa told of how, in the first two years of Chaucer, she and Nick went to every single meeting organised with the local Health Authority, just to keep on their good side. When they look back at their notes, what they see is that, despite hours of talking, next to nothing was achieved.

Of course she, along with all the staff at the Clinic, accept unconditionally that their business, every business, has to operate within a regulatory framework. But regulations weren't the issue.

The real problem was the misinformed idiocy behind those regulations, and the petty bureaucrats, the pensions-in-waiting, who enforce the rules to the letter, but who have no conception of the spirit behind those rules.

I was told of one particular idiot who refused to talk to anyone from Chaucer, or even reply to their letters. The reason? A Chaucer staff member had inadvertently used the wrong title when addressing him in their initial written communication. The affronted officious official wouldn't even write back to correct the error; instead he chanted the self-important bureaucrat's mantra: "Ignorance of the rules is no excuse!" Then there was the time when the plight of a young girl was brought to the attention of the clinic. Nick telephoned to seek special permission to see the child who was obviously abusing booze.

The clown of a civil servant who took Nick's call replied: "You are exaggerating. There are no fourteen year old alcoholics. They can't even drink until they're eighteen." On yet another occasion one jobsworth insisted that there were too many right-handed doors in the Clinic; imagine a department that checks on discrimination against left-handed doors! The fact is that many inspectors go out of their way to find something to complain about. That is, after all, how they prove to their masters that they are doing their jobs.

Only just recently a Social Services group from the Midlands came down to Chaucer to discuss placing some clients at the Clinic. Nick, Teresa and Nikki set aside the whole afternoon for the meeting. The party left home two hours late, and didn't arrive until after four o'clock, messing up the whole afternoon for the Chaucer team, who had to rearrange at short notice meetings arranged for later in the day.

The visitors showed no consideration. It didn't even occur to them to phone ahead and let Chaucer know they would be late. Obviously it meant nothing to them that everyone at Chaucer was kept hanging around. It was gone eight o'clock before they left. Most of the visit was spent discussing details about the Clinic's procedures, most of which the visitors should have already known, since they had been sent numerous Chaucer documents prior to the meeting. On one of those documents it is stated quite clearly that Chaucer doesn't accept anyone with severe psychiatric conditions or a history of arson. It just happened that one of the men they wanted to place was a convicted arsonist; a fact only disclosed a long time into his assessment. Chaucer naturally refused to take the man, and the visitors went away complaining that their time had been wasted, when they themselves were wholly to blame.

Thankfully not every official the Clinic deals with is so petty, bloody-minded, vicious, stupid, single-minded or insensitive. This is just as well since there is a minimum of ten inspections annually, from 'Health and Safety' to the Fire Brigade - many of them unannounced. There are a few delightful, helpful, kind, and constructive individuals who help Chaucer through the minefield of officialdom, and for which Nick and the gang are eternally grateful.

Careless in the Community

In one conversation I made the mistake of casually mentioning 'Care in the Community' to Teresa, and was treated to a firework display as she exploded in an incandescent fury. The first few years of Chaucer had been extremely successful: bed occupancy was high and success rates very gratifying. The Clinic was more than paying for itself. It was all going so well - too well! But then the social programme, euphemistically labelled 'Care in the Community' (lack of care was closer to the mark), was launched on an unsuspecting Britain in April 1993. Everything changed.

This progressive (!) legislation changed the structure of government funding of care centres. Patients were pushed out of institutions into the community, where they were to receive any medical treatment as outpatients. The effect was that large numbers of 'mental homes' closed down, and institutionalised mental health patients (including many alcoholics) were flushed out onto the streets. The tip of this massive iceberg was (and still is) seen in the regular headlines of the British press telling of vagrant psychopaths randomly murdering unsuspecting passers-by. Less visible, however, are the numerous stories of suffering among the human detritus.

Apparently it was all for the greater good of the patients. According to the politicians, the patients would now have a choice (Hobson's Choice more like: take it or leave it), with friendly assessment procedures and a clear intervention and rights policy. Lies! It was all about saving money! Perversely the programme ended up costing far more, not only in the human misery it caused, but also in money that the state was supposed to save.

At the time it was generally accepted that the resources of the national Social Security budget were being stretched to the limit and beyond, with widespread waste and abuse (financial and physical) in the system. Of course something had to be done, but all that 'Care in the Community' achieved was to throw the baby out with the bathwater. Britain's alcoholics along with many other unfortunates were washed away in the flood. The 'street population' of the major cities soared, as the pathetic dregs of society with 'no fixed abode' disappeared from official view, thus losing any support and entitlements from local authorities. Such patients could only be accepted on programmes like Chaucer's when funding was made available. However, the general attitude of bureaucrats was that the homeless were someone else's problem, and consequently any request for money was most often refused. Even on the rare occasions when funding was forthcoming, the consequential bureaucracy behind the decision-making had soared, in effect eating up a larger proportion of the declining resources.

All Change

Thus it was that from 1993 everything changed. In the following decade, right up to the present (New Year 2005), Chaucer would operate as a loss-maker. Although Nick, the Marauders, and other Chaucer staff and members would have numerous hilarious adventures and misadventures over that period - enough for another book in fact - the real story of that period is how the Clinic kept going against all the odds. There would be many occasions when I asked Nick if he could keep Chaucer going? The sensible business decision was to close down. Indeed, there was one particular moment in the late nineties when Chaucer was haemorrhaging money so badly that some trustees and senior members of the staff held their 'Last Supper' and decided to close down the Clinic.

Driving away from the meal, with Teresa, Nikki and Kelly sitting disconsolately in his car, Nick received a telephone call from the family of a drunk begging for help. Without a second thought, the team immediately swung into action, phoning around fixing up the required help. It took a few minutes before Teresa realised that they were still on automatic pilot, reacting instinctively to SOS calls. She started laughing: " I think we've just changed our minds." They were committed and just couldn't walk away. If Chaucer needed money then they would find it elsewhere. They would ignore the sensible business advice to cut and run: "when you're in a hole, stop digging."

Nick always believed his guardian angel would come through for the Clinic. Perhaps that angel is Harry the Hat, looking down benignly on them all; after all Harry still owes Nick half a packet of cigarettes. There was one occasion (one of many) when the money ran out, only for them to receive a cheque for £12,000 in the post, from a local authority who said they had been undercharged for services rendered. Another time they were staring into a financial void, when out of the blue, singer/songwriter Paul Simon sent $10,000. In fact the list of Chaucer's spontaneous donors reads like a who's who of pop music: Eric Clapton, Phil Collins, Mick Jagger, Pete Townshend and Roger Waters to name but a few.

Therefore, it is hardly surprising that Teresa's anger peaks when she talks of the bureaucrats and their political masters who never see "the pitiful plight of an alcoholic motivated to seek treatment. In their humiliating and desperate battle to gain a place in a rehabilitation unit, they are in torment and despair. There is no publicity for these no-hopers, no supporters willing them to succeed. Their begging and pleading is met mostly with the same response: no money, followed by doors slamming in their drunken tear-stained faces." There is no pity on offer. The bureaucrat, the representative of society's attitudes, smugly says it's all the drunks' own fault. The unspoken attitude is 'do us all a favour ... just go away and die.' And die they do in huge numbers, although the causes appear on the death certificates as heart attacks, strokes, suicides, brain haemorrhages, trauma from road traffic accident etc. How ironic that the tax-take from alcohol that causes these deaths goes a long way to pay the inflated salaries of these no-sayers to any help.

Teresa says that society is in denial. It wants nothing to do with the casualties of alcohol, the legal and profitable (5% of the country's tax revenue), and yet lethal drug. Starved of cash, and bested by the uncertainty caused by 'Care in the Community,' clinics started to close down all across Britain, and consequently the number of beds available nationally decreased dramatically. The few clinics that managed to survive had to be finance led, which meant appropriate treatment took a back seat as services, facilities and length of treatment were slashed in the rush to balance the books.

As all around them other clinics were closing, Chaucer still managed to survive. This was because it was run like a business, but never as a business. Nick has always resisted the temptation to compete with the luxury addiction units (like the Betty Ford Clinic in the U.S.A.) that cater for rich and privileged clientele. Such clinics can welcome (and usually re-welcome many times), and provide instant treatment to every celebrity applicant who has fallen off the wagon. Nick doesn't see himself lying to health insurance companies that the drunks in his clinic are suffering from stress, just so that the treatment is paid for.

Chaucer just has to survive, because Nick's approach works. Who else is going to help the many penniless failures at Alcoholics Anonymous who are desperate to kick the habit? Patients dependent on handouts from the Department of Health and Social Security (DHSS) are envious of the rich drunk, who receives treatment in less time than they spend waiting to be served in the local 'offy' (off-licence). Nick, on the other hand, with Harry the Hat whispering in his ear, can never forget the typical and less fortunate alcoholic. If this means that Chaucer's income stream makes the enterprise unviable, then Nick just has to dream up some entrepreneurial scheme to cross-subsidise it.

Smoke and Mirrors

Britain's social services, in their economy drives, have developed a similar tactic. The apparent savings that they claim to have made with Care in the Community were, in fact, illusory. For they too were being cross-subsidised, and the 'savings' were the result of the real costs being transferred elsewhere, to the National Health Service (NHS), probation service, courts, prisons, police departments, housing offices and charities, not forgetting the biggest money pits of all, business and society in general. Figures published in 2002 by 'Alcohol Concern' showed British industry losing   around   £3   billion   annually   through   absenteeism, unemployment and premature deaths as a direct result of alcohol abuse. The cost of treating drink-related illnesses by the NHS should be added into the equation, not forgetting the treatment of misdiagnosed alcohol-related ailments, as well as picking up the pieces of road accidents and all the other violent crimes that involve alcohol. One in five male patients admitted to general medical wards have alcohol-related problems, with the fraction much higher in Accident and Emergency departments - with a consequential higher incidence of assaults on nursing staff. One third of all accidents, half of domestic violence, two thirds of all murders and of all suicides are the result of drink. Most alcoholics only get a bed in hospital for a secondary, though alcohol-induced condition, such as attempted suicide, an injury incurred when drunk, or when the alcoholic is close to a drink-induced death.

Nowadays, what little state funding there is available is targeted at narcotics and not alcohol. And why? Drunks tend to harm themselves and close family, but to the general public they are seen more of a nuisance than a threat (although there is a high murder rate, and who knows what automotive carnage they cause?) Junkies, however, are trouble, because in their drive to fund their habits, they are likely to embark on various forms of property crime. Furthermore, because booze is legal, the government needn't be seen to do anything about the problem, but ignoring illegal drugs would be a dereliction of duty.

Teresa cannot hide her fury at the sheer waste of it all. "The irony is that the total cost, when all these service providers are accessed, far outweighs the cost of long term rehabilitation placement. If allowed to proceed without the tills ringing at every point, clients can successfully leave rehab having used fewer resources. Then they can return back into the system as useful members of society - as earning and tax paying citizens." This de-concentration and spreading of expenditure into many different cost-centres may very well appear to balance the books, but it's all just 'smoke and mirrors,' and does nothing to eradicate the basic problem. It simply diverts and postpones the inevitable. Because of the misconceived attempt at social engineering, projects offering rehabilitation services were driven into crisis, and were closing daily. Morale amongst providers hit an all time low. Quite simply, Care in the Community failed the alcoholic, but it also failed the community. However, nobody in authority cared. "Society likes to drink, dislikes the troublesome drunk, and ostracizes the alcoholic." Heaven help the next generation of alcoholics, which is already in full-time training "on the piss, most likely in a children's playground near you!"

Doctors at Sea

Against this background it's not surprising therefore that both Nick and Teresa's attitude towards authority is highly ambivalent. When they respect the individual wielding that authority, then the pair is highly supportive. However they believe it is essential to question everyone, particularly the 'experts' as well as the administrators and regulators, whose actions tend to conflict with their own sense of what is sensible. Consequently Nick, in particular, is often at odds with many in the medical profession; Teresa tends to be more diplomatic. Of course the medical profession itself has more than its fair share of drunks. Nick recalls one occasion in Chaucer One, when a doctor was called to a member who had an alcohol seizure (a type of epileptic fit). The locum arrived and was halfway through the treatment when he too collapsed in a heap ... with an alcohol seizure!

Nick says there are (sadly, quite a few) pompous doctors who really don't know what they are doing when it comes to treating alcoholics. Yet they manage to hide behind the authority of the medical establishment, all the while forgetting the responsibility they bear. Seven out of every ten drunks who check into Chaucer have been prescribed anti-depressants by their doctors. The Clinic's policy is to withdraw that medication. Alcohol is itself a depressant, and so of course alcoholics are depressed. Anti-depressants simply treat the symptoms, not the underlying cause: alcoholism. Nick refuses to stand idly by when a further chemical cosh is administered to a person already bludgeoned by alcohol abuse. If authority and responsibility are not aligned, the result, in the hands of well-intentioned fools, is an abuse of power. Nick has no patience with people who are all theory but little or no experience, are not open to novel ideas, and all the while refuse to get involved.

Baby Blues

A heavily pregnant Irish girl was one of Chaucer's early members, and while Nick had no intention of turning her away because of her condition, she was admitted to the Clinic with a great deal of trepidation. Would they be able to cope when 'the time came?' Sure enough, nature followed its course, and during the early hours of her third morning at the Clinic she went into labour. But they had no transport! Just then Nick heard the rattle of milk bottles. Problem solved! 'Phil the bottle,' their local milkman, whisked her off the few hundred yards down the road to hospital on his milk-float, leaving several crates of 'gold-top' on the side of the road. She gave birth mid-afternoon.

Driving past the hospital on his way home a few days later Nick saw the mother, sitting on the fire-escape outside the ward, knocking back a bottle of something. This proved to be only the first of several sightings. Then word came through the grapevine that the baby was having trouble. Soon afterwards a doctor from the hospital rang up, asking for Doctor Charles. Nick explained he was not a doctor, but the heavily accented enquirer didn't seem to understand. He was too busy telling Nick about the highly distressed state of the infant. It seemed that the mother had refused to breast feed the baby. Did Dr. Charles have any advice? It seemed clear to Nick that the baby's problem was not the mother's lack of interest ... the poor mite was suffering withdrawal symptoms. The baby had become addicted to alcohol while in his mother's womb, and was now missing the booze.

Nick suggested that the mother initially breast-fed the baby on every other feed, and then every third feed, gradually over time reducing the amount of tainted milk in the baby's diet. His last piece of advice was to insist that the mother continue her regular drinking pattern until the baby was completely detoxed. Then the mother (and baby) could be returned to the Clinic where she could complete her treatment.

A second doctor contacted Nick a few weeks later fascinated by this successful approach to the problem, asking if he would write it up in the hospital newsletter. Nick said he was only too pleased, but wished to make it clear, as he always did when dealing with medics, that he was not a doctor, but the director of Chaucer Clinic. The medic recoiled in horror at the thought of the life of a child being entrusted to a non-medical man, and only begrudgingly admitted that Nick's action had undoubtedly saved it. Nick heard nothing more about the article.

More Doctors at Sea

Doctors, predominantly General Practitioners, regularly ring up from far and wide to ask how Nick could possibly consider himself qualified to criticise their methods. However, he remains adamant that treating a drunk is not the same as treating a sober human being. Addiction and withdrawal add a whole new dimension, a totally new layer of complexity to the symptoms of the patient, which in turn makes any diagnosis highly problematic. Nick used to argue this point of view directly with doctors, and more often than not it would end up in a slanging match. Nowadays he knows better; he's realised there are jobsworths in every profession, and he is wasting his time trying to convert them to his "unqualified" position.

More recently Nick has reached a much wider audience with his increased exposure on radio, television, and in the press. On these 'chat shows' he is often dismissive of the official initiatives concerned with (say) the rough sleepers on London's streets. He says that the regulators have no conception of what's happening at ground level. They may be aware of the vileness of drunks and junkies, but they have no understanding of them. That is why the political agenda is to sweep the problem under the carpet, all the while deliberately confusing the issue in a snowstorm of statistics aimed at denying that there is even a problem.

Nick frequently finds himself at the wrong end of a barrage of official data, harangued by some pompous official insisting that figures don't lie. His response is to quote Mark Twain: "It's not the figures lying that concerns me, but the liars figuring." Nick is intrigued by how, and by whom, the data was collected? Sober civil servants or university researchers, although well meaning, are not the best people to collect data on the homeless. Many 'street people' are addicts of alcohol and narcotics, and/or are mentally unstable. Only those researchers not frightened by addicts - and addicts can be very frightening - should collect the data. Nick has his suspicions that many data collectors don't dare to venture down the dark and threatening streets where the drunks and junkies actually congregate, but instead go to more convenient, and safer locations.

Nick is gradually getting his message across that there is a crisis on our streets and that, as he shouted after Harry the Hat, "something must be done about it." When he was awarded the MBE he was very gratified to receive in excess of a thousand accolades, many from the medical profession. Slowly but surely the opposition is receding, and nowadays the general reaction to his message is begrudging acceptance of the work of Chaucer, although he still gets resistance from certain quarters.

Rumours

His situation today is so very much better than in the early days of Chaucer Mark One, when it was non-stop grief. This was particularly the case with the staff of other alcohol units. The nursing and ancillary staff at the Max Glatt Ward of the nearby hospital were vociferous in their objections to Chaucer. This was hardly surprising because Chaucer was charging a mere £260 per week for each bed, whereas the statutory ward was levying £1250 per week. With such an enormous difference, the staff at Max Glatt began to worry that their ward would be closed down, and that they would lose their jobs. The trade union got involved, distributing leaflets that urged hospital workers to picket Chaucer in order to "get them out." They simply refused to accept that Chaucer could offer a better service at a fraction of their price.

Amazing rumours began to circulate to the effect that the Conservative Government of the day, as part of a conspiracy designed to undermine and then replace expensive facilities in the statutory sector, was secretly funding Nick. Apparently Chaucer was part of a plan hatched by cynical politicians; workers in the public sector saw Nick's programme as a first attempt at privatising their jobs. However, when this nonsense gained little or no credence outside a small circle of activists, the stories about Nick became more and more extreme. It all ended in farce with them spreading the fantasy that he was a drug baron, with a yacht anchored off Cannes in the South of France, and that he was using the Clinic only as a front.

There followed an amazing catalogue of dirty tricks that lasted for the first four years of the Chaucer's life. Literally every department in the Health Authority and Local Authority receiving scurrilous reports, many of them anonymous, of Nick's malpractice. The ludicrous gossip reached such a fever pitch that the authorities could no longer ignore it; with the result that Chaucer was being investigated ad nauseum. Since none of the crazy allegations had any substance, each soon faded away. But the annoyance continued with a procession of inspectors of every kind tramping through the Clinic: hygiene, health and safety, gas, water, electricity, followed by bankers and auditors. The only problem they uncovered was that it hadn't occurred to Nick and the senior management team of Chaucer that they should be paid wages; they only took expenses. Nick and the gang were obliged by the inspectors to pay themselves nominal salaries in order to comply with various regulations. On another occasion the Health Authority sent inspectors to check the administrative system that Teresa had developed. However, far from discovering any malpractice, the auditors recommended that many of the ideas she had painstakingly developed should be used in the main hospital!

Regulations Gone Mad

The Chaucer team bravely managed to cope with the malice; at least they could understand the reasons behind the aggressive behaviour aimed at them. However, they will never understand the mindless, arbitrary and sometimes spiteful actions of bureaucracy, problems that have been gaining momentum during the new millennium, and which seem to be getting much, much worse. In April 2002 the power to inspect Care in Community regulations moved from the Social Services Inspectorate to the National Care Standards Commission (NCSC). Every time a new broom appears on the scene, a huge amount of resources goes up in smoke. This particular change led to an even bigger bureaucratic muddle than usual. Managers in care homes across the UK, be they housing children, the infirm, the elderly, or addicts like Chaucer, all had to be officially licensed by 1st July 2002, and staff had to be cleared with the Criminal Records Bureau by that deadline. Staff members employed by schools were also included in this regulation. The authorities set up a telephone help line to deal with enquiries, and around nine thousand residential homes called in. The call centre just couldn't cope, so the deadline was extended to August. Their problem was further compounded, when, at the beginning of that month, two young schoolgirls Holly Wells and Jessica Chapman were murdered in the Cambridgeshire village of Soham by the school caretaker Ian Huntley. Public anger reached fever pitch, and the vetting of all workers in schools was given top priority.

This meant the residential home sector went to the back of the queue whenever officials had to respond to the many queries about the regulations: the spin of government targets was focussed elsewhere. It was total chaos. The letters sent out to residential homes gave the wrong phone number for the 'hot line.' Then the date when all staff had to be reviewed was moved to March 2003. That date too came and went without even the necessary application forms having been printed. This caused even more phone calls, and a further waste of time, energy and money.

Of course all new staff have to be vetted! Jim, who applied for a job at Chaucer, when asked if he had a criminal record, didn't bat an eyelid when he replied, "rape, buggery, but only when I was drunk; oh, and I'm on the sexual offenders register." He didn't get the job! There is a real and ever-present problem in protecting the innocent from 'Stranger Danger.' However, the fact is that in drug and alcohol centres many of the counsellors are reformed addicts, with criminal records (admittedly not as serious as Jim's) gained while under the influence of their particular poison. Replacing these active and committed workers with do-gooders with no direct personal experience of alcoholism, even if such workers could be found, is a huge mistake. Some of Chaucer's most enthusiastic and inspirational employees are unemployable elsewhere, and government regulations would end up forcing clinics to discriminate against these people; the complete inverse of the original intentions. And does Chaucer really need an abuse policy in which they must state that they have checked out the milkman? The situation had become farcical when Chaucer was refused permission to employ a new manager, not because of any shady past, but because his licence was not forthcoming. The reason? The bureaucrats at the Criminal Records Bureau had fallen too far behind processing the paperwork.

If only the problem was about staff being trustworthy! Highly placed interfering busybodies also insist that Chaucer staff must pass paper qualifications to 'prove' they can do their job. Those in the counselling and caring professions must obtain an NVQ (National Vocational Qualification) level 2, while managers and secretaries require a NVQ in business administration. This is a ludicrous audit mania: targets gone mad. Nick himself must have a NVQ level 4. Even worse, do-gooders who have never confronted a knife-wielding drunk are always telling him that he must "communicate" with violent clients and not show aggression. Nick knows exactly what to do with this 'touchy feely' advice, although he is probably breaking a hundred and one regulations in the process. "The purpose of Chaucer is to treat drunks, not to be sensitive about their feelings, not to worry about paper qualifications; and certainly not to count the number of showers in the bedrooms, or right-handed doors."

Furthermore, under the present regulations Teresa is obliged to produce an alcohol policy stating that no alcohol must be consumed on premises: what lunatic dreamt that up? At the same time another official questionnaire wanted to know if there was a bar at Chaucer, and how many people used it! Then there must be a policy that ensures whistle blowers are not penalised. What a pointless exercise: "Drunks don't grass." The authorities insist that unemployed members must be actively looking for jobs, whereas the Clinic requires them to be totally involved in the Chaucer programme. Furthermore the official line is that Chaucer is not allowed to coerce members into joining in the activities: they must have the right to choose. But work therapy is just that - therapy, and members do not have a choice about whether or not they receive treatment.

Going, Going, ... Gone

There are all sorts of spatial requirements being placed on all residential homes. The regulators seem to have no idea that different client groups (kids, the elderly, the sick, drunks) have different requirements. Infirm elderly patients benefit from a large bedroom, however, alcoholics spend most of their day in communal areas, and only 'crash' in their bedrooms; most of them are also used to Salvation Army hostel dormitories and any personal space is a bonus. Who knows what might have happened following an application on behalf of two Siamese twins from Africa? The Clinic did have a single vacancy, but would the authorities have insisted on them occupying separate rooms had they been admitted?

New standards have been imposed for the minimum width of doorways, to allow for the easy movement of wheelchairs. BUPA, the private health company, found that the doors in their clinics were two centimetres narrower than the standard. It didn't seem to have occurred to the bureaucrats who devised the standard that wheelchairs have no difficulty getting through the doors of BUPA hospitals - buildings that after all were specifically designed to allow for the free movements of patients. BUPA would have had to spend millions of pounds widening their doors, before another document appeared stating that the figure given was only a guideline, and not statutory.

And why did the regulations become mere guidelines? After all, under the spate of regulations the government was in sight of actually achieving its stated objectives. Certificated saints would staff every care home in Britain, with clients sleeping in large spacious bedrooms, complete with en-suite bathrooms. How was this utopia possible? The only homes left in business would serve a celebrity clientele who paid through the nose. As for the rest, they were closing down in droves. Implementing the new regulations costs huge sums of money, and the profit margins of most care homes were not sufficient for the banks to agree the loans needed for the renovations. The increased administrative costs alone were enough to drive some homes into bankruptcy. The private care sector was in meltdown, and the public sector already overstretched would have to take up the slack. The officials were forced to give up their ridiculous regulations for otherwise the government would have been forced to step in and bail out the whole sector - a very expensive option.

Being a shrewd judge of character, and cynical of just how parsimonious government can be, Teresa's policy has always been to wait and see; ignore implementing all special standards until official deadlines made it absolutely necessary. "If you jump at the first approach of bureaucracy, you will spend all your time jumping." She has seen so many colleagues in the health sector put enormous effort and expense into completing paperwork well in advance of a deadline, only to find that everything would change at the last moment, and all their efforts counted for nought. In November 2002 Chaucer was visited by an official delegation, and nothing the Clinic did was acceptable. Teresa pointed out the futility in their regulations to the inspectors, and they went away. She sat tight and the same group returned in March 2003, by which time all the regulations had changed. Following this visit Chaucer was officially given a clean bill of health. Experience has taught her that over the past decade most regulations turn out to be mere draft recommendations, not officially imposed, and there is no guarantee that they will ever be enforced. Teresa was now in full flow: "as it stands at present Chaucer will become illegal in 2007 because of spatial requirements. With all the problems we face, Chaucer could go bust ten times over by then; so 2007 can wait. I'm not going to waste our resources worrying about something that may never happen." No she wasn't psychic - the authorities subsequently scrapped their demands on space for existing properties!

A new inspectorate body, the Commission for Social Care Inspection (CSCI) took over in April 2004, a combination of the original Social Services Inspectorate and the NCSC, together with a new third organisation thrown in, who no doubt would completely rewrite the regulations again. They are more bureaucratic than ever, insisting on an excess record keeping - the pre-inspection form takes Teresa over a week to complete!

Does anyone in authority have the slightest idea of what is going on? The systemic nature of doing business is that it is complex, and the ever-increasing body of regulations is making it even more complex. Despite all the fine words, the actions of successive governments demonstrate a total lack of coherence in the way they approach the problem of alcoholism. Entering the new millennium, the New Labour government claimed to have a drug tsar - but he didn't look at alcohol, the biggest drug of all. He was an ex-policeman to boot, which meant no self-respecting junkie would talk to him, and anyway he soon resigned showing up the whole scheme to be a shoddy public relations stunt. The intention of allowing 24-hour opening hours for licensed premises will have the benefit, as government sees it, of increasing the tax-take from alcohol sales, but the problem of alcohol abuse can only get worse. All in all, the situation looks totally chaotic.

In a 2001 document published by the Greater London Alcohol Advisory Service (that now no longer exists), Prime Minister Tony Blair told of his government's alcohol strategy, and yet on the other side of that very same page, one of his ministers said there was no such strategy. The National Alcohol Strategy, or rather the Alcohol Harm Reduction Strategy did finally arrive, albeit six years later than promised. However, it focuses on prevention, harm reduction, education, awareness etc. particularly among underage drinkers, but the question still remains: who is going to pay for treating the vast numbers already abusing alcohol? Apparently there is a plan to "carry out a national audit of the demand for and provision of alcohol treatment services, to identify any gaps between demand and provision." So that's all right then! Let's hope that it too isn't six years late.

Of course it is good to focus on prevention and reduction, but while governments are busy strategizing, funds for treating alcoholics have all but dried up. Local authorities, GPs, statutory services, independent providers are being stretched financially to their limits, and beyond. As the government is slowly deciding on how to pay for treatment, services are closing down through lack of funding, and the treatment sector is losing valuable, experienced workers.

12

Darkest Before Dawn

Having survived the ill effects of so many regulations that were strangling others in the care sector, despite myself, in irrational moments I was beginning to wonder if, after all, Chaucer had a charmed existence, and that Harry the Hat really was smiling down on them. However, slowly but surely the cash flow began to dry up; inexorably Chaucer was running out of money. The day finally arrived when Nick found out that he couldn't pay the salaries of his staff. Never one to give up without a fight, Nick, with Kelly's full support, raised a £60,000 loan against the value of their house, and stopped taking a salary for themselves. Teresa and Nikki did likewise. In this way the rest of staff would be paid every Thursday, cash on the nail. The injection of cash meant that the Clinic had sufficient funds to keep going for a few more months. By pulling in their belts, perhaps, just perhaps, they could make it through to better times. After all, in the past when things got really bad, Nick's lateral thinking would switch in. So it was only a matter of time before he sorted it all out!

Then disaster struck! In January 2002, the law concerning charities changed, and threatened to destroy everything Nick had worked for during his years of sobriety. From that date all charities were obliged to declare their accounts; failure to do so within six months of the year-end became a criminal offence. Nick was totally unaware of this change, and even if he had known he would still have been unconcerned. His long time friend and even longer time accountant had everything in hand.

Let's call the accountant Tom; it's as good a name as any. For as they were soon to discover, nobody at Chaucer ever knew his real name. They were all blissfully unaware that many years earlier

Tom had turned Queen's evidence against some seriously heavy villains, and had been given a new identity and relocated under the Witness Protection Scheme. Tom's latest dishonesty would lead Nick to Bow Street Magistrates Court, where he "was to stand in the same dock as Crippen and Lord Haw Haw." (The former was a wife murderer and the latter a traitor).

A Betrayal of Trust

The situation was extremely serious. At this time I had known Nick some seven years, and I had hardly ever seen him depressed in any way. Despite his outward devil-may-care appearance, Nick has a deep respect for Authority, and he craves their respect, which is why the award of the MBE meant so much to him. When the full impact of the charges hit him, he was pushed to the edge of despair. He felt a shame, much deeper than when he was a dosser.

Only after "it hit the fan" did Nick discover that he was totally responsible for ensuring that the accounts had been submitted to the authorities; and that responsibility had not been met. Being a Trustee of Chaucer, it suddenly dawned on Nick that technically he was guilty of the offence. Nick released the Chairman of the Board of Trustees, who was nursing a sick wife at the time, from any blame. Nick accepted that he alone was answerable for leaving everything to Tom, and so he, Nick, took full responsibility. He would carry the can; and Tom of course, who was guilty anyway.

Tom, on whom Nick had unknowingly pinned so much faith, had once been an employee of the Charity's original accountants, a firm with impeccable credentials. Then some years on Tom had announced that he was leaving the large firm and setting up on his own. Would Nick like to move his account? The larger firm didn't seem to object because his wasn't a very big account, so Nick agreed.

The years went by, accounts appeared on his office shelf, and all seemed well, that is until 2002 when the Fraud Squad turned up. Somewhat embarrassed they asked for the Clinic's tax returns. A bemused Nick went to his shelf, helpfully handed over what he had, and then told the police they should contact his accountant, who would sort out the obvious misunderstanding. This was when Tom's deceit started to unravel. It turned out Tom wasn't even qualified, and Nick along with a number of Tom's other unfortunate 'clients' had been duped. It seemed the police had an inkling of this, but they had a job to do.

During his time at the large accountancy firm, Tom was merely a ledger clerk fantasising about being an accountant. Tom's new accountancy company never submitted any accounts to the tax authorities because in doing so Tom would have been caught out in a lie. Until 2002 it didn't really matter, but the change in the law dropped Nick right in it. Was Tom a Walter Mitty character, or an out-and-out crook? Nick never got to the bottom of that particular question. He just wanted to draw a line under the whole shameful exercise. Although guilty of the charge, the judge recognised Nick's naïveté in trusting a charlatan, and Nick was given a nominal fine. Nick had thought his accountant was a friend, and that you trusted friends, but he had been caught out by the first rule of the confidence trickster: "Cheat family and friends first."

Nick wouldn't be caught out in this way again, and has since appointed Les Newman, and Lucy his accounts assistant, from a highly reputable firm of accountants based in Norfolk: Newman and Co. When he eventually emerged from his gloom surrounding this debacle, ever the pragmatist Nick told me: "It doesn't matter how dark it gets, darkness is useful. You find out who your real friends are: whom you can trust, whom you can rely on, and who stands by you. As a drunk I learned all about fair weather friends, why should my being sober make any difference?"

The Wishing Well

As a drunk Nick had spent many an hour in court, and never once felt the slightest shame. Sober, however, he was mortified to be in this position. Previously Nick was never one to lie there licking his wounds. Normally it wouldn't take long for him to pick himself up from a setback, dust himself off, and start all over again. This time it was different. He was shaken to the core, and very stirred by his ordeal.

Following the judgement, day after day Nick sat staring into space, in the depths of despair. For the first time in his life Nick's self-confidence had deserted him. Where was Harry the Hat now that Nick needed him? Not that far away, as it happened. Kelly, Teresa and Nikki were in Nick's office, trying (and failing) to cajole him out of his gloom, when they heard shouting coming from the Annexe garden. They all rushed out to hear Stan Wilkins, "effin' and blindin'." Stan, however, was nowhere to be seen, although one of his boots showed above the ground, entangled in the roots of a tree.

Nikki had sent Stan out to plant a new rose bush as part of his work therapy. He had dug a nice deep hole and was surveying the scene. Stan had stepped back, onto an inspection cover that was shaded by an old tree that dwarfed the garden. He was about to fill in the hole with a mixture of compost and bone meal that would give the plant the very best start in life. But it was not to be!

The ground started to shift beneath Stan's feet. A huge hole appeared. The inspection cover, large chunks of earth, together with the rose bush plunged deep into the bowels of the Earth. Stan too fell headlong into the hole. Luckily for him, his boot became trapped in the tree's roots, the very same roots that over the years had gradually undermined the inspection cover. He was left dangling there, very lucky not to have joined the rose bush on its trip into Hades.

With everyone laughing heartily, they eventually pulled Stan out. Nick peered gingerly into the seemingly bottomless pit. It was very dark down there. He sent for a torch, and shining the beam into the depths he could see old brickwork and water - a lot of water. Stan had only just avoided plunging headfirst into a well. Tossing in a fifty pence piece, Nick made his wish, delighted to have received his sign from Harry the Hat. In that instant, and despite all his misfortunes, the Old Nick was back, more determined than ever to turn it all around.

Nick knew about the 'well' in Han'well' since first coming to the site. The hospital had been built on the site of the old Hanwell Asylum. Water had been drawn from this well since before the Romans, but this fact had been quietly forgotten in these modern times of hot and cold running water. Scouring some old plans of the site, he located an entry. Nick ignored the "Danger, do not enter" signs and climbed tentatively down the rickety steps to an amazing sight: a small room with mosaic walls housing a mini-reservoir fed from a well that was cleansed each day by hundreds of thousands of gallons of fresh spring water.

The Hanwell Asylum used this water to brew its own beer, of a quality renowned across London up until Victorian times. Here was the ultimate irony: the Chaucer Clinic for alcoholics was sitting on top of a huge well of water that in a bygone age had serviced, of all things, a brewery! Here was a sign, if ever he needed it, that life is full of perversity. Nick had come through his ordeal. Once again he was convinced that the only way was up.

Nick the entrepreneur sprung into action. If the fresh spring water could be used to make beer, then it could be used to make ... fresh spring water! Why hadn't he thought about it before? Pint for pint, bottled water was retailing at more than petroleum. He would bottle Hanwell water and make a fortune. Of course he knew nothing about the bottled water business, but that didn't stop him saying: "I can do that." Nick went into overdrive, and in no time at all he had had the water tested for purity. Then he went out searching for investors among his network of contacts, all the while reading up on the water business and planning an extraction and bottling plant.

Money Laundering

This wasn't the first time Nick had toyed with the idea of selling Hanwell water. A few years earlier a rather strange character had strolled into his office asking to see the well, dumping a canvas bag containing £50,000 on his desk. The man wanted to buy a directorship in Chaucer, not realising that it was a Charity. Teresa was particularly suspicious after their previous dealings with people offering to give them money. The discussion became animated, as she demanded to know more about the would-be benefactor, so much so that nobody noticed Winston walk into the room, pick up the bag, and walk out. Nobody noticed because Winston, a pensioned-off printer originally from Antigua, spent his days wandering around the Clinic picking up laundry bags. The strange thing was that, although Winston enjoyed doing the laundry, he wasn't very good at it, as he never seemed to get the clothes really clean.

Anyway, the heated discussion gradually fizzled out, and looking down at the desk they noticed the bag had gone. "Winston!"

shouted Nick and Teresa in unison, and with the visitor close on their heels, they charged off to the laundry. They arrived to see the bag of money, surrounded with soapsuds, spinning around the drum of a front-loading washing machine. The bag was rescued; and the money, sopping wet and reeking of soap powder, was handed back to the stranger. But at least they found out why Winston never got the clothes clean. He used to throw the laundry bags straight into the washing machines without first taking out the clothes. With the clarity of hindsight, Nick observed: "I don't know why we're surprised. To Winston it made perfect sense. Remember the time when he was overhauling his printing equipment, and he put all those greasy and oily components into the washing machine?"

The mysterious stranger turned out to be an entrepreneur in the bottled water business, and a bit of an amateur historian. He had tracked down the Hanwell-well, and saw a business opportunity. He eventually told Nick about his plans, but at that time Nick wasn't convinced. The poor man died a few weeks later in an accident, and the whole episode just faded from Nick's memory, that is until Stan's escapade brought it back with a jolt.

Alcoholism - The Social Disease

Nick's flair for enterprise was back in overdrive. Out of the blue he had struck oil, or rather water. However, as he began to find out more about the water bottling business, a very unwelcome fact reared its ugly head. If he were going to bottle the water, then Chaucer would have to close down! The necessary production facility would need all the space presently occupied by the Clinic. On the back of this business plan Nick could easily raise the money to buy the site, and they could move Chaucer elsewhere, but it would be sad to walk away. Nick didn't want to move, but if the long-term future of the Clinic could be made secure, then so be it!

No longer gloomy about Chaucer's survival, entrepreneur Nick was off and running. Those who know Nick, realise that he has never restricted his energies solely to helping the small proportion of drunks who manage to reach the doors of his clinic. He has a much bigger agenda; he wants to inform the whole world of the dangers of drink. Nick has certainly opened my eyes. As a life-long tee-totaller, I must admit that my attitude towards the netherworld of alcoholism was, and still is, far from sympathetic. Nor do I have any time for sentimental 'do-gooders,' who in my experience do more harm than good. However, Nick has made me recognize alcoholism as an increasingly disruptive social phenomenon that is being dealt with against a background of shrinking government resources.

He points at the Greater London area as a magnet for 'drop outs,' leading to a self-perpetuating and expanding sub-culture of alcohol and drug abuse. Large swathes of British inner cities are seedy and unpleasant, with begging 'dossers' littering up the pavements. Unless the country can break out of this vicious circle, then many parts of our larger towns face a dire future. For the pressures of 'globalization' and of 'new technology' are such that wealth creation will be concentrated in 'economic hot-spots': localities, suburbs that are pleasant places to live, work and most importantly spend. However, the 'cold-spots' will be abandoned to despair. Evidence of this can be seen in the 'no-go' areas of towns like Liverpool, where even the major banks have pulled out, leaving these communities to their fate.

There is an ever-growing number of drunken, often violent and abusive vagrants littering our streets. Many of these drunken misfits are adolescents, and younger. They have run away from home to escape the violence of drunken and abusive parents. Furthermore, the pressures on these young people are enormous, and they are going to get worse. Youth unemployment, particularly among young males, is a serious concern. Because of the fear of failure - no, the expectation of failure - amongst youngsters, and a total lack of hope, many are sliding slowly towards drink and narcotics. Drug addiction may get most of the headlines, but whatever the newspapers say, alcohol abuse claims far more casualties than narcotics, and is often the entry point for drug abuse.

Nationally, the emphasis is all wrong. Schools focus their attention on narcotics and ecstasy, because these drugs are illegal. Booze, however, is far less frightening. It's everywhere. It's part of the culture. 'We did it, so it's only natural that our children do the same.' Unsurprisingly, very few see the scale of the problems, such as the smokescreen that is the blitz of 'alcopops' advertising targeting naïve and impressionable kids, which ends with 'binge drinking' becoming the norm. Our society has demonised tobacco, why not alcohol? "Why is it that tobacco companies are the bad guys, but not the booze companies?" With his confidence back, Nick was going to do something about it.

Certainly my own personal stereotypical view of the alcoholic has been shattered completely. Talking with Nick and his staff, seeing what they have done in the Chaucer Clinic, and meeting some of his 'members,' has made a profound impression on me. These members, drawn from across the full social spectrum, had been dragged down to the depths of degradation. I saw the appalling damage, sometimes permanent, that alcoholics inflict on themselves, and this experience has, if anything, made my fear for the future of this problem in our society even more acute.

However, at the same time, I see hope in the Chaucer Clinic, the institution that journalist and writer Simon Beckett ironically called "the last chance saloon." What I see is NOT the lowest common denominator of shared misery that is the usual portrayal of meetings of alcoholics. I see self-help not self-pity, self-discipline not self-denial. I see inspirational leadership that fosters commitment and loyalty, and an infectious enthusiasm from Nick and his staff that instils hope and confidence in the future.

There is a real sense of community at the Chaucer Clinic, which engenders a trust in the clear message that there is a way out of alcohol abuse: Nick Charles is himself a prime example of that fact; and he leads by example. There is a positive sense of action, and through that, Nick re-instils in his members a sense of self-worth. Nick, his staff and members all radiate an aura of success that is contagious. And they do it all with hardly any help from a society unwittingly facing alcoholic meltdown.

Education, Education, Education

A firm believer that prevention is better than cure, Nick is now intent on tackling the thorny problem of how to educate the medical profession in particular, and also those sections of society that are at particular risk of sliding down the slippery slope of alcohol abuse. Specifically he has young people in mind. Over the past few years, the behaviour (in relation to drink and drugs) of their role models from the worlds of sport and entertainment is far from exemplary. Nick is determined to reverse the trend.

In order to get his message across to a wider public Nick blitzes the media. He's never off the telephone to the newspapers, using his public relations skills to disseminate his message about the dangers of drink, as well as promoting the Clinic and its staff. Consequently Nick has become the first point of reference for reporters who want an informed comment on alcoholism and alcoholics. Nowadays, hardly a week goes by without some celebrity or other hitting the news-stands over an alcohol related problem, and that means Nick is rarely out of the media spotlight.

When his book *Through A Glass Brightly* - a sanitised version of the 'diaries of Brummie Nick' - was first published by Robson Books in 1998, Nick did hundreds of radio, television and newspaper interviews. To his annoyance he had to organize most of the publicity himself. In fact Nick was so dissatisfied with his lack of exposure by his publishers that he decided: "I can do that;" and not just the publicity. He would do the publishing as well! For some time Nick had realised that he would need a publishing house for all the educational material he wanted to produce. The mainstream publishers weren't interested; not enough profits. So Nick bought a dormant publishing company - using Kelly's Visa card! He would do it all himself, but in such a way that it would not be a major drain on the Chaucer's resources. He found a reliable printer in Ebbw Vale in South Wales, and the books and pamphlets produced would be warehoused in the Clinic, and the staff would do the telephone sales, as well as the postage and packing as part of work therapy.

A new realisation is also driving Nick. He's getting older and has started to worry about what will happen to Chaucer when he dies. I really mean die, and not retire - for he'll never retire. He says he has come to realise that in its present form he is Chaucer, and when he goes Chaucer will close. From where I stand, Nick has got it the wrong way round: he should close Chaucer down, before the Chaucer money-pit closes him down. However, Nick wants his mission to continue, so he's thinking of franchising his methods. His educational programme has to be formalised and published. Naturally enough, established publishers are not interested in such a project with its limited financial returns. With his own publishing company, however, Nick had just the vehicle he needed to spread the word.

Nick set about publishing a wide range of educational pamphlets, including his six-week test: a simple way of testing, over a six-week period, whether the reader is 'merely' a heavy drinker, rather than dependent on alcohol. That dependency can go unnoticed, even to the drinkers themselves, because they never stop drinking. Nick insists that anyone who goes into a bar more than 4 times a week, and for more than two hours a time, is very likely to be dependent. Once a body tolerates excessive consumption, say drinking twice the accepted level (up to 21 standard drinks per week for a man, 14 for women), then it has become alcohol dependent.

Those dependent on alcohol have to be medically detoxed to get off the booze, or eventually it will kill them. But not all drunks are pub drinkers. Nick cites a man who looked down on boozers - both the pubs and the drunks. He never went to the pub, but he would drink brandy in his coffee, both morning and afternoon. He would swig bottles of lager with lunch, and on his tube journeys to and from work - not realising that he too was a drunk. Drunks are more than capable of deluding themselves as well as their nearest and dearest. Hence Nick's determination to raise awareness of the problem.

Beyond Chaucer

Nick is not satisfied with just looking out for the drunks in his Clinic. He wants to help the many more drunks in the community. He is convinced that hundreds of thousands of Britons are dependent on alcohol; he avoids calling them alcoholics. Nick sees his role as going far beyond Chaucer, to a general education programme that warns the general public, particularly youngsters. I am not alone in thinking that Nick's time and energy would be far more effectively spent in prevention for the many, than on a Clinic that can treat just a few: but he will hear none of it. He has run projects for schools, telling children of the dangers of drink. He even managed to get the Queens Park Rangers football team to give match tickets, and Middlesborough FC to donate signed footballs, as prizes in 'The Schools Cup,' a programme run on the Internet aimed at involving both children and their parents in his alcohol-awareness schemes. Unfortunately, it was singularly unsuccessful, but Nick won't be giving up just yet.

Far more successfully, Nikki runs a telephone help line, and on the Internet they are hosting www.addictionnetwork.co.uk with advice for anyone and everyone who has alcohol-related concerns. This site regularly attracts 200,000 plus hits every month, and rising. Nick is also keen that the medical profession become better informed of the dangers of drink. Misdiagnosed alcohol dependency wastes scarce resources. Nick gives examples of people who go into hospital for treatment (say for appendicitis) and then inexplicably get 'the shakes.' He knows of one doctor who tested a patient for malaria, when the real reason was withdrawal symptoms. Hardly surprising when over the many years doctors spend qualifying, they usually have little more than a single lecture on alcoholism.

Nevertheless, Nick is slowly gaining credibility among the medical profession. At the time of writing he is preparing a speech for a major medical symposium, and he is talking to Professor Graham Neale of Imperial College London with the view of medical undergraduates receiving the benefits of Nick's teachings.

Nick's successful foray into publishing has whetted his appetite for the media. He's even dragged me into his plans, having me talk, successfully it seems, to film writers about turning his life story into a movie. What is more, Nick has paid for an option to buy a Sky satellite television channel. He has big plans that mix his contacts in the entertainment business with a business channel, and he has brought together a potential group of backers. Quite unpretentiously he says that he has only given a new twist to his original idea of bringing Northern Club acts to the London pub entertainment circuit. It looks like all systems go.

The Big Deal

Nick is back on song. The schemes and deals are bubbling again. As usual in his entrepreneurship, Nick started thinking 'outside the box,' just like he did on the streets. He isn't exaggerating when he says, "every tramp has to be a successful wheeler-dealer. In that hand-to-mouth existence it makes the difference between life and death. Failure means you have to try something else, or starve; there is never the choice of doing nothing." Not surprisingly, Nick doesn't differentiate between big and small deals. They're all deals, and he wants it all. "And who knows? That small deal could open the door to something much bigger!"

And very much bigger it has become! The schemes just keep coming. One day he had a visit from Kevin McGrath, a vice patron of Chaucer, who permanently sponsors a room at the Clinic. McGrath is a big time property investor, who buys shopping centres - not just shops, whole centres! Not satisfied with planning the water deal, Nick thought "why not ask Kevin if he had any ideas to help raise money for the Clinic."

Kevin smiled benignly and sensitively pointed out that "Chaucer wasn't a viable business. You don't save an unviable business, you normally close it down!" Of course Kevin knew that that particular option was out of the question, indeed his financial support was key in keeping Chaucer going. He agreed with Nick's suggestion that he would see if there was any mileage to be made out of Chaucer's property portfolio.

Nick said: "there's no time like the present," and grabbing Kevin's arm, walked him all around the property, namely Linden House, and F Block next door. "Of course," said Nick, "you do realise both are Grade 2 Listed Buildings." This meant there would be problems over demolition and re-development. "And there is the minor detail that I don't own any of the buildings!"

Kevin's brain went into overdrive. The germ of an idea was forming. He could see a way of making enough money to fund the Clinic in perpetuity, but it too would involve moving the Clinic. Rather than bankruptcy and closure, was Chaucer Mark Three beckoning?

The best deals are win-win situations, possible because the different sides in a deal have different perspectives, different requirements, different priorities, and different constraints on action. On the face of it, Chaucer had very little to deal with, but the trick is to use information to leverage what little you do have.

Nick had learned through the grapevine that the government had asked the hospital authorities to build a 60-bed regional women's secure unit and a 24-bed adolescent centre in their grounds. The £80 million development, to be paid for by the Department of Health, involved knocking down both the boiler house and the laundry.

The development would abut both Linden House and F Block, but the two buildings were not part of their plans. They couldn't be converted into anything useful, and they couldn't be demolished. Nick was led to believe that as far as the hospital was concerned these two buildings were liabilities. English Heritage had slapped a Grade 2 Listed status on both, which meant any development would have to leave the integrity of both buildings intact: a big problem. In fact, by occupying Linden House for more than a decade, Chaucer had been doing the hospital authorities a huge favour by maintaining the fabric of the building. If the authorities asked Chaucer to move now, after so long in residence, then they would be left with the thorny possibility of compensation, as well as the continuing problem of maintaining the fabric of Linden House, and not just F Block. With a malicious grin, I nudged Nick: "if the hospital authorities give you any grief I'd go to Brussels, trumpeting the Human Rights Act? That'll tie them up for years. You've been at the wrong end of regulations for long enough. Why not give them a taste of their own medicine?"

Such a potentially huge development on the hospital site means finding low-cost housing for the large number of new staff (250) needed to run the facilities. Surely there is no way that the hospital would want to get involved with supplying accommodation for their shift workers? If Nick could somehow square this particular circle then Kevin could broker a deal. Armed with only his wits, the insight that public sector managers are always on the lookout for low-cost solutions, and his large network of contacts, he started planning.

Nick and Kevin were joined by Maurice Fitzgerald, Philip Little, and Harold Winton, business associates of Kevin, and together they set about costing and evaluating an idea. Chaucer would buy Linden House and F Block, and convert them into housing: part low-cost for the staff, part up-market apartments for management. Kevin's firm would undertake the conversions, obtain the funding, and the property itself would be run by Chaucer. The proposal would have to come through Chaucer, because they recognised that Chaucer's agreement to moving out and relocating locally was likely to be a major factor in getting both planning permission from the Local Authority, and the agreement of the Health Authority Committee members. Both Local Authority and Health Authority had government quotas to obey, and the continuance of low-cost Chaucer in their jurisdictions was very useful in demonstrating best practise in the various quality audits that an overly bureaucratic government machine tended to impose.

How would the Health Authority, in particular, take to the idea of Chaucer becoming a multi-million pound property company? Teresa invited the Health Trust members to a meeting with Nick, Kevin and associates, and tentatively laid the deal on the table.

The Fat Lady Stays Silent

What a difference a year makes! Nick seemed to be in a position to secure Chaucer's future by moving into the property business, or by selling bottled water. "Amazing! It's like waiting for a bus. You wait for ages for one to come along, and then two appear at the same time."

However, what was Nick's reaction to this incredible turn of events? "The show isn't over 'til the fat lady sings." He was hopeful that one of these deals would make Chaucer secure, but he wouldn't really believe it until the ink had dried on a contract. That is why he hasn't given up on the small deals: "You never know, I may still need them. And anyway, that's what I do. I can't just switch off." The big deals could still all go wrong ... and go wrong they did!

It was all too good to be true. The Trust was under extreme pressure to complete the secure unit as quickly as possible. However, the logistics of them making it all happen, particularly housing the staff, would become an insurmountable obstacle. Affordable accommodation in London is non-existent. Kevin and Nick were offering the Authority a solution in which they would gain substantially from the deal, and at the same time avoid any costs linked to Chaucer. All that was left was to agree a price and obtain planning permission. All three groups would make a profit. Chaucer would own the property, and the rental income would subsidise the Clinic; the developers would be paid a reasonable profit; and the Hospital Trust would have their problems solved and get a good price from the sale of the land.

It was all too good to be true. Nick's trusted allies in the hospital, Abdy Richardson erstwhile Chairman of the Hospital Trust, and

Eddie Kane, its Chief Executive, had long ago moved on to pastures new, and the present Trust members, despite all the transparent benefits of the property deal, had other plans for F-block. They were prepared for Nick to sign a new lease on Linden House, but that was all. Nick, Kevin and colleagues had spent a great deal of money developing the plans, only to find that they had been encouraged by an administrator who was outside the power loop, and had no authority to act.

What about the water? That too was a pipe-dream. The authorities filled in the well - no doubt claiming 'Health and Safety.' Anyway, the sheer scale of transporting massive amounts of water off the property would have met with objections from all sides: the Local Authority and Hospital would claim that the domestic roads were unsuitable for the operational traffic; and English Heritage would object, because that's what they do.

The Professor and the Tramp

I was amazed with Nick's equanimity. All his plans had gone up in smoke. Once again Chaucer's future was back in jeopardy, and yet there was no hysterics over what might have been. His response was "I'll just have to think of something else."

It was nearing the year's end, 2004. The book was more or less complete. Nick's story was completely up-to-date, or as up-to-date as a biography can ever be. I had told how he has travelled to hell and back: from being a down-and-out living in a sewer, to the giddy heights of multi-million pound deals, but then back to a more mundane reality of the small- to medium-sized enterprise.

But it couldn't just end there, with Nick wheeler-dealing off into an unknowable sunset with the intention of keeping Chaucer going against all the odds. I had given Nick the text of the book, albeit still short of a suitable punchy ending for the book. Perhaps Nick would have some ideas? Hence, I was particularly interested in his opinion of the final chapter (chapter 13 that follows) where I analyse his way of doing business.

His response? "Strange! Is that how professors think? Very strange, but interesting! I'd never have thought of what I do in that way." And then he went very silent, waiting quite a few minutes before asking: "is this the sort of thing you talk about in your business lectures?" Nick knew that over the past decade I had given over a hundred presentations and after-dinner speeches on the international lecture circuit.

A long drawn out "yeh-ess" was my suspicious reply.

"Do you think those audiences would be interested in what I have to say?"

There followed my even more suspicious conditional affirmation. "I know my students are interested in your approach to management, and a general business audience likewise - that is, after all, why I wrote this book in the first place. They'd be keen to hear you talk, but on motivation. Over the years I've shared the stage with some most uninspiring 'inspirational speakers,' so I'm sure you'd be a knockout. Don't, whatever you do, go on about the evils of booze. That's a real downer. Audiences, particularly after-dinner ones, tend to be 'well-oiled.' They don't want to be preached at."

"Great! That's decided. We'll be a double-act. I've even got a title for the talk: 'The Professor and the Tramp.' You can be the straight man. What do you think?"

Something told me I had just been bounced onto a rollercoaster ride! But I was still short of an ending.

13

Bringing It All Together - Nick's Management Style

This book started as an analysis of Nick's management style in response to requests from my students at the London School of Economics. Only during the writing, did I veer off, and end up writing Nick's life-story. Therefore, it is only appropriate at this point that I bring the book back full circle to consider his business approach. Having spent most of the previous pages recounting his anecdotes, it is now time for me to make sense of them by showing how these far from spurious stories have actually had a formative influence on Nick's attitude towards business.

During our collaboration on this book I have got to know Nick and Chaucer very well, and I now feel competent to comment on his abilities and character, and on those of his colleagues. So what is Nick's business secret? Does he have a secret? After ten years of regular conversations, and having written the previous twelve chapters about him, I feel I am in a position to second-guess him. It is time to confront Nick with my analysis of how he does business. I couldn't wait to see what he would make of my comments!

Here I was giving Nick my considered analysis, all the while he was keeping me informed as he was balancing his various deals and projects. Would his schemes bring Chaucer back from the brink, or could they even push him over it? Personally, I had absolutely no doubts that Nick would continue as an entrepreneur, however, my grave doubts of the viability of Chaucer remained, as I would tell him many times. Nick and Kelly had become my friends, and I didn't want to see them on the road to ruin - but then, what does a teetotal academic who experiences business second-hand know? Either way I was in a position to bring together all the strands of his operational thinking, and to deliver some fascinating material for this final chapter. It would mean that I would have to take a little longer in completing the book, but these new conversations would validate my grasp on his business strategies.

Now our conversations were no longer about Nick's past, but of his future. I pressed him about his unconditional financial support of Chaucer, about his management style. We talked about the autobiographies of famous businessmen, in which captains of industry laid out sanitised self-perceptions of their personal management styles. With a self-deprecating shrug, he immediately discounted their relevance to his position.

"I don't get carried away with big deals. I'll believe it if and when it happens. As far as I'm concerned I run what you call an SME, a small- to medium-sized enterprise. What can I learn from the stories of 'Neutron Jack' Welsh or Bill Gates or Rupert Murdoch? Theirs is a totally different world. If I'd played at being the big businessman, or acted like the alchemists in the book you showed me by Charles and Elizabeth Handy (*The New Alchemists*, Hutchinson, 1999), Chaucer would have gone bust years ago."

Ungraciously, I interrupted Nick with a reminder that it can still go bust. Unabashed he continued: "businessmen like me face totally different problems from the big boys. I'm not running a large business, with major investors, credit ratings, share-options and the like. The rollercoaster of the past couple of years should have shown you that. With me it's more like hand to mouth. I ask you, what big businessman would re-mortgage his house, or refuse a salary, in order to keep the firm afloat?"

"SME's are not about money and profit. Like every owner of an SME, my approach has had to be different. I learned long ago that the management techniques developed by and for big business don't scale down. SMEs are totally different from large corporations, and they must be run differently."

Then, with a twinkle in his eye, and ever the optimist he added, "but who knows, if things go well, maybe this time next year I'll be a big corporation! But for now I'm still a small-scale entrepreneur. I buy something for a penny and sell it for tuppence, but without spending another penny. Running a clinic like Chaucer is more a vocation than a job. My purposes and priorities have to be radically different."

However, as much as he likes to deny it, it's not quite that simple. Nick's freewheeling days have long gone. He didn't approach the water or land deals as a small-time player. Furthermore, even without those deals, he has the thankless task and huge responsibility of running Chaucer in what is an increasingly regulated and cash-strapped environment, and that pressure (not to mention Teresa breathing over his shoulder) must inevitably cramp his freewheeling style. The staff and the members of the Clinic, damaged by booze, are all relying on him. There can be no more hand-to-mouth operating whilst bearing such heavy responsibilities.

So in what strategic direction was he taking his business? "Strategic what?" When I described the concept of strategic management to Nick, and told him about Michael Porter's five competitive forces, and value chains, supply chains, of the works of Peter Drucker, Kenichi Ohmae, Mintzberg, Ansoff, and the thousand and one other management gurus, Nick seemed singularly unimpressed. "Don't they all play for Chelsea!" He thinks such high falutin' ideas have very little place in the running of a small business like his, and he adds that he isn't totally convinced that they have much place in big business either.

"I don't believe in planning for the future by pretending I can imagine what will happen, and thereby control what are, after all, unknown and unknowable business risks. With Chaucer I look at the world in terms of what I'm trying to do. I focus on my core aims, knowing who I am and what my driving purpose is. That means trusting in my insight, and having faith that I can ride the onrushing tide of events."

When I think of Nick, archetypal images inevitably come to my mind. One of the strongest is of Nick as the little boy in the crowd, ridiculing the Emperor's suit of clothes. He has a jaundiced take on methodolics, and everything I have told him about management methods - or the lamp-posts, as he now calls them. "Method is the last (in fact the only) refuge of the mediocre."

Nick keeps asking me, with just a hint of malice, whether the people who 'ponce' around with their strategic plans ever look back to see whether last year's plan, or even last week's, actually achieved anything. He quotes Winston Churchill: "However beautiful the strategy, you should occasionally look at the results." "And how much does it all cost? Too much probably, which is why I bet they shy away from spending yet more money to find out that they have achieved very little with their daft ideas." Nick is probably a little too close to an uncomfortable truth when he asks: "do they strategise just because that's what senior managers do. It just makes them feel good as if they are in control: when in fact it's all bunkum."

However, he's not fooling me. In watching him over the years I have seen nothing haphazard or arbitrary in what he does. Despite outward appearances, Nick's approach is to focus his problem-solving can-do mentality on a portfolio of experimental projects, each supported by insight rather than by process: that is his strategy. And I stress strategy, and not strategic planning. "Strategic planning? That's a delusion; real strategy is enterprise, thinking outside the box, and positioning yourself to take advantage of the situation - any situation. We cannot plan the future; the best we can do is to prepare for it. As we wade around, knee-deep in the uncertainty of business, our actions send ripples out into the world. There they conspire with the actions of others. Most dissipate, but some return to us in a flood of both opportunity and hazard. In the torrent of feedback, two and two adds up to whatever you want it to be." Forget methods and planning. Only those with a state of mind imbued by a sense of wonder can take advantage of the opportunities, while at the same time avoiding the hazards. I am struck by how, in his approach, the lessons Nick learned as a drunk now seem to help him deal with the 'downers' and the inevitable problems of business, and how they inspire in him an unshakable faith in his own abilities, and a belief that something will always turn up - and it usually does.

Nick's Golden Rules
So far in writing this book I have been painting Nick's portrait, describing what he has done, but never how he did it. Now is the time to confront Nick with his personality, and with what can only be called his coherent strategy. As I see it, that strategy is driven by a few fundamental ideas:

- Never bet your shirt on any one big project; always have a whole portfolio of (dozens of) small plans on the go at any one time. Never get so tied up with one particular project that it blinkers you, and hinders you from being simultaneously involved with others.
- There is never a shortage of opportunities out there. Follow your nose, and the smell of a deal. Accept or reject a project after asking yourself "would I put my last pound on it?"
- Always be ready to start a new project, even if you know very little about the particular business sector. However, whatever business you find yourself in, always do your homework; and talk to people who know. Don't misunderstand this approach with amateurism. There is no room for dilettantes in business. Expect to do huge amounts of background investigation, and employ the best professionals to support your projects. But make sure those professionals have real experience, and not just mere theoretical expertise.
- Most importantly trust in yourself, and in your own insights.
- Get the cash flow right for each individual project; Nick regularly talks about 'cost plus 20%' (see below); always make a profit. Never keep going in the vain hope that it will eventually pay. Be objective: never become personally involved - Chaucer excepted, as I keep reminding him!
- Make sure there are plenty of reality checks; never get carried away with your own cleverness. Always have someone else who has a major say over the money, and the right of veto (in his case Teresa). In this way the more lunatic ideas are strangled at birth. (Teresa saves Nick from going bust once a month, and from drowning in his own euphoria at least once a week.)
- Be sceptical. No deal is ever done until it is signed, sealed and delivered, and the monies paid.
- Always read the small print; and be ready to walk away and write off your investments.
- "Management is solving what problems you can, but only when they find you." Don't go looking for trouble, and don't overcomplicate. 'If it ain't broke, don't fix it.' Most problems will go away of their own accord. Fretting about problems only amplifies them.
- Only trust those people who have earned that trust; never be surprised by how low humanity can go, or how high.
- If you have been let down, learn from the experience. Never let it happen again.

- If you can't trust them, make sure they need you more than you need them; at least until you've got what you wanted.
- Remember it's not just you doing the innovating. Everyone around you is at it. Make sure that they know you expect their support, commitment and help. Gradually build up relationships, and from those networked relationships come opportunities. Share the rewards equitably among the network.
- Personality is more important than process. You cannot replace the talented and committed individual.
- Beggars can't be choosers; take help from wherever you find it. However, don't expect to form long term relationships with businesses whose managers are not totally committed to their company. If they aren't loyal to their employer, then don't expect your wishes to factor into their decisions. Such managers cut and run, and never look back at the chaos they leave behind. Their successor is likely to be equally disloyal, and this 'new broom' will sweep you aside without a second thought.
- You must be scrupulously honest, or you will be found out, and then honest people won't want to know you. Every drunk has learned that lesson the hard way.
- The world is full of fools, many of whom work for the government. Always work around them; if you meet them head on then you will pay dearly.
- Don't let the downs stop you from getting up again; you can only learn from failure.
- And last, but not least, go with the flow, and never lose your sense of humour.

However, with this list of bullet-points I don't mean to give the impression that Nick sits down and aims these rules at each business opportunity that comes along - he is no methodolic. What I have described above is more the consistency I have observed in the consequences of his actions. This consistency is NOT the intention behind Nick's decisions, it is not how he does it, rather a side-effect of the essence of what he does. No leaning on lamp-posts for Nick. He is convinced that very often the taking of a decision is far more important than the decision itself. "In business, standing still means you're losing ground." The inertia of indecision is more damaging than a poor decision! So Nick's 'rules' should be seen as just my perception of the effects of his subconscious predisposition to decision-taking. Note effect, not cause - and it's always a mistake to mix up cause and effect.

Breaking the Rules

These rules are apparent in the way Nick managed his hairdressing salons, in how he worked the Northern clubs, and how he ran his string of 'exotic' models, the London pub circuit, the theatrical publicity, and even his brief entry into boxing promotion. On the very few occasions when Nick broke his own rules, he has very nearly come to grief. He had trusted Tom, his accountant, and look where that got him. After so many years, Nick had thought that Tom had earned his trust. Nowadays he knows better than to bestow his unconditional trust on anyone: apart from Kelly, Teresa and Nikki of course.

Nowadays Nick is obsessive about reading the small print. When he was running the pub entertainment circuits in London, a huge amount of paper was pouring out of the office. Printing and photocopying was a nightmare, so he undertook a leasing contract with Xerox. But he didn't check the details! The moment he signed on the dotted line he was in it for five years, come what may. When the pub circuits went belly up, he still had to pay Xerox. At one point in 1986 he was in hock to Barclays Bank to the tune of £97,000 and ten pence. The bank manager called Nick in and told him he had six weeks to pay up, or the bank would seize their house. Nick had broken one of his golden rules. He had borrowed money to buy the equipment needed to expand his business. When the contracts were suddenly withdrawn, he was left with useless equipment, and a big debt.

It was because of this cash flow crisis that Nick first got involved with theatrical public relations. Three jobs in quick succession each netted him "10% bums on:" that is 10% of profits over and above a quota. He was paid in cash every Friday. Coming up to the bank's deadline he still owed £10,005 and ten pence. Then the final cheque for his promotional work on his last production popped through the letterbox, for £10,005 and ten pence, a sure sign that "somebody up there loves me."

This was just one of many other occasions since, that they had nothing in the bank. Once, Nick needed to borrow £1000 to open the Clinic on St Bernard's, so he went to Barclays Bank. There he was refused the money as being un-credit worthy, despite having paid off all his previous loans in full. He immediately closed his account, and went across the street to the Nat West Bank where he got his loan. Nat West will get all his business from his future deals, despite attempts by Barclays to win him back. Barclays let Nick down once; it won't happen again.

Following The Rules: The Café on The Green

When Nick and Kelly left the Northern Club circuit they decided to open up a café in the park in Hounslow, quite near to their house. A number of people had previously tried, and failed, to make a go of the site that was owned by the local Council. Nick managed to negotiate a lease in that he would pay a percentage of turnover. He then did a 'back of an envelope' calculation in which the café was to bring in "costs plus 20%."

Nick worked out just how many cups of tea, hot dogs, sandwiches, soups etc. he would have to sell in order to stay on the right side of the formula. He very soon realised that his present clientele was not large enough. Nick pored over Yellow Pages to find all the companies in the vicinity, and then sent Kelly around them all selling sandwiches.

However the market was still too small, so he decided to target local school children. Why? Because the odd truant would drop in to the café to buy coffee and sandwiches, and to listen to the pop-music on Nick's radio. A regular theme of their conversations was the poor quality of school dinners. Ever the opportunist Nick told them that if they and their friends paid him their 'dinner money,' he would feed them burgers etc., and all the while they could listen to the latest pop-music. Within days the café became the regular lunchtime haunt of hundreds of school children, and not just the truants. In fact, he was so successful that the head of the local secondary school visited the café to complain that the numbers taking school dinners had collapsed.

Nick always works with low overheads. With the café, whenever there was a surge in demand, drunks from his day centre would be wheeled in to help. In inclement weather these volunteers could always be relied on to put up tarpaulins, so that what was previously a seasonal business, and limited in profitability, could now run the whole year round. With his low cost base Nick knew exactly what he had to achieve in order to turn a profit. There would always be the occasional marketing and logistical problems, but Nick has a total belief in his ability to solve such difficulties. But if problems ever proved insurmountable he would just walk away, not having spent too much of his capital in the scheme. Managing it in this way, the café became a goldmine, at least in the short run.

He stuck to his list of rules, limiting the investment in the café. For example there was no on-site telephone (this was in the days before mobile phones), so the business was run from their home. Kelly would make the sandwiches in the kitchen, and while there she could take phone calls. She would pretend they were running a highly organised business. In a cut glass accent she would say "Hello Charles Miller Enterprises. May I help?" "Oh you want the café? Please wait." Kelly would then simulate the sounds of various dialling tones "beep, bop, bap, bap, beep, bup, bop .... " and then in a 'common' accent screech "Allo, Caf 'ere. Wad'jer want luv." She would take the orders and then leg it across the park with the order for sandwiches or whatever.

Eventually the Health Regulations changed in respect of catering. The authorities demanded proper fitted kitchens. It no longer made economic sense to Nick. He knew the local "toe-rags" would break in and steal his investments. So he cut his losses, and gave up the cafe.

As one door closes another opens. Nick started organising the pub circuits. He went to the local Osterley Hotel with an offer for putting on entertainment in the pub. "I'll do the lot for £120 per week." Nick calculated the price by working backwards from what he needed to run the business, and adding 20% - not complicated arithmetic. He wasn't aiming at megabucks, just a sensible and reasonable profit, on the basis that "survival plus a little profit" will usually deliver competitive prices. Whatever the scheme, each project has to pay for itself over the short term, but Nick will cut and run whenever the projects don't pay. He pulls the plug and moves on to next idea; just like the artistes who joined Nick on his pub circuits - they too realised that variety and the Northern Clubs were dead and it was time to change.

The Other Nick

However, there are two Nicks: the entrepreneurial Nick with his rules, and then there is Chaucer Nick. Nick, the entrepreneur, uses a scattergun approach, juggling lots of business deals at any one

time. This is how he makes his own luck: the scattergun.
Generally his deals are self-funding, with a little up front
spending that he is willing to write off. The trick is not to be
greedy. Nick usually steers clear of the big deals with their
concomitant long-term investments. He doesn't think about
winning big, and in that way he never loses his shirt. Each deal
has to make a reasonable profit, and Nick views them all as
having a limited lifetime. He kills each one off before the
inevitable diminishing returns starts to drain away accumulated
profits.

However, when almost by accident, Nick sleepwalked into
creating Chaucer, he threw his rulebook out of the window. With
Chaucer, Nick totally ignores his guidelines. Here success is not
measured in terms of money. Chaucer is the reason he is in
business, not the business he's in. He doesn't find new ways to
make money out of Chaucer, but for Chaucer. Chaucer is a
monster he created, and can't give up - I regularly remind Nick of
what happened to Frankenstein because of the monster he
created. If Nick had walked away (a la rule 8 above) from this
money pit in the early 1990s, cutting his losses at the time of Care
in the Community, he would have been reasonably well off, rather
than finding himself mortgaged to the hilt, and living off credit.

He doesn't see himself abandoning the Clinic, and what he has
come to regard as his life's work: the project! Chaucer is not a
business; it really is a vocation. But at what cost! Of course he tries
to limit the costs and maximise the profits whenever possible: or
rather to minimise the losses. However, Chaucer's survival is
never brought into the equation. I keep telling him that one of
these days the economic realities will catch up with him. Until
that fateful day he expects to cross-subsidise Chaucer from all his
other deals. He dares not calculate how much of his personal
wealth he has given to Chaucer, never expecting it returned: it
must be hundreds of thousands of pounds. So quite naturally he
views the assets of Chaucer, such as the products of work therapy,
as part of those deals, which can and should be used in synergy
with his other projects. It has been this way since he first formed
his day centres, and nothing has changed.

Builder Jim McReady from Hayes was buying baths from Sean
O'Farrell. They were Victorian and made of cast iron, scrounged

from the derelict buildings on the site. The builder would then re-enamel them, and sell them for a large profit in London's Docklands. Once on a visit to Docklands to do a newspaper interview, Nick took the opportunity to see McReady's building site and inspect some completed flats. They also had Victorian style cast iron radiators that had to be imported from France. Nick asked how many would be needed for the whole site. Two thousand. "I can do that." He scoured the derelict wards, which were in the process of being demolished, refurbished the old radiators in 'work therapy,' and then sold them for half the French price.

Whenever Nick has an idea, his first task is to find out what he doesn't know. He then works out where to go among his large network of friends and contacts to find the expertise and information needed in order to put the deal together. He approaches the targets in his network with such charm and energy that they find it impossible to say no. I myself have learned that Nick always gets his way, and so it is quicker (and cheaper) to give Nick what he wants straight away. But he is never unreasonable in what he asks of his contacts. Consequently everyone enjoys the ride, and so they keep coming back for more.

By now it was clear to me, and hopefully it is clear to the reader that Nick lives on his wits, and by his wits; he doesn't run his life by a schedule. He has a surreal view of the world, where anything is possible, within reason. Just like 'Bugs Bunny' in the 'Looney Toons' cartoons, when others believe the rabbit has painted himself into a corner, Nick paints a door on the wall, opens it, and escapes. He uses his imagination to create a different room, a different situation. His actions do not contradict the constraints of the old room where he is trapped, but by choosing to view that situation differently he has a different set of choices, and hence a different set of opportunities opens up for him.

The Fat Lady Sings?

With the previous section, my analysis of 'managing uncertainty the Nick Charles way' was complete. But I still had the problem - how to end the book. It was December 31st 2004 - New Year's Eve. At around ten-thirty in the morning my phone rang: "Ian? It's Nick. I've got an ending for you. Pop over."

Nick, Kelly and Teresa were sitting on the sofa, faces sombre. Nick came straight to the point: "We're closing Chaucer! Nikki agrees. We're in a deep hole. It's finally time to stop digging. We were counting on £30,000 per month for the next quarter from a charitable foundation, but we were told this morning that the money has been withdrawn, and sent instead to South-East Asia for the tsunami tragedy appeal. We just can't go on with the thankless task of subsidising the Clinic. The regulations are making it impossible for us to do a good job. It's driving us crazy. We're at the end of our tether. I've got to think about our futures. You've been warning us for years that we would eventually reach a point when we would have to cut our losses. This is it! We know it makes sense. I can't tell you what a load this takes off my mind. The girls too. Tonight I'll have my best night's sleep in years."

I couldn't take it in. I knew their resolution made good business sense, but still I couldn't believe it. I sat there in silence for over an hour as Nick and Teresa went over, and over, and over their justification for the fateful decision. For the past six Christmases I had witnessed the four of them agreeing that this was their last year, and yet come each January back they went. They had never before sent texts and e-mails of their intentions. This time the fat lady really was singing - the show was over. Could this really be the end? Had Harry the Hat finally deserted him?

What a Difference a Day Makes

Happy New Year, 2005! I had my conclusion, but it was not the one I had hoped for. So, it was all over! Thoroughly depressed, I felt that writing those last few paragraphs could wait. I resolved instead to escape, and spend New Year's Day in front of the television. Thus it was, one hour into Liverpool versus Chelsea, that I heard a loud pounding on my front door. Nick charged in, followed closely by Teresa. "So Nick, I gather you've now decided not to close Chaucer!" I said with a smug grin on my face.

Nick stood before me, brimming with energy and confidence. He had just lost a major source of funding for the Clinic, but he would just have to go out and find more money. He had done it before, and he'd do it again. Nick winked, and in a booming voice announced: "All aboard the Skylark! Hold on tight, we're in for another bumpy ride."

Back from the brink, yet again? How typical of him, I thought, and how well it summed up the book. Finally I had a fitting end to my telling of Nick Charles's tale: the story of how a dosser, a down-and-out, the lowest form of life, pulled himself out of that mire, and every other quagmire since, by sheer force of an indefatigable will ... and who knows what other Force?

But it wasn't to be. Always one to learn from experience, Nick finally realised that keeping Chaucer Clinic afloat was actually interfering with his long-term goal of getting his treatment more widely accepted. Chaucer haemorrhaged money - a quick back of an envelope calculation showed Nick that he had poured well over a million pounds of his own money into the black hole of the Clinic. What is more, "I finally realised that I cannot hope to heal the world when I am focused on treating the thirty odd alcoholics in the Clinic." Hence, and after much soul-searching, on April 4th 2005 Nick, Kelly, Teresa and Nikki decided to close down Chaucer. On April 5th they launched the first viable on-line alcoholism treatment programme. Chaucer Clinic's twenty-six week, four-part rehabilitation course is now available to everyone worldwide:

www.alcoholismtreatmentonline.com.

Postscript

This book is finally finished. It has been a long journey from our very first meeting, when Nick offered to show me *The Diaries of Brummie Nick*. Middle-class politeness was the main reason I agreed to read them. Although, if I am honest, it was also to a certain extent my morbid curiosity about this wisecracking larger-than-life character who had come to live next door. In this unpromising frame of mind I started reading. I was not expecting much, envisaging an uphill struggle through tedious self-pitying and self-justifying anecdotes of a then-alcoholic.

But his diaries were a revelation! As a life-long tee-totaller, I must admit to a non-existent knowledge of alcoholism and the nether world of the alcoholic. In fact the whole alcohol experience was completely foreign to me, as was any form of drug abuse. At the same time I was forced to recognize alcoholism as an increasingly disruptive social phenomenon in today's Britain; alcohol, because of its legal status, is probably more disruptive and sinister than narcotics.

So it was, exhibiting another middle-class characteristic of having little or no patience for those with self-inflicted wounds, that I began reading Brummie Nick's diaries. I fully expected to be irritated by Nick's descriptions of how he fell out of 'normal society,' and his inevitable futile repeated attempts at re-entering it. And irritated I was. I couldn't manage to trawl up the slightest compassion for his predicament. Quite the opposite in fact: I found my biases were firmly reinforced.

What I did not expect, however, was to be gripped by the story. My stereotypical view of the alcoholic was completely shattered.

What I read was not the ramblings of some 'dosser' whose brain was addled by booze. What came over, crystal clear, was the logic of the alcoholic, the logic of an alien mind, a demonic mind. Nick had somehow managed to capture that internally consistent yet warped logic in his writing. The narrative of his journey into the underworld of the alcoholic vagrant was truly compelling. And who knows, perhaps Nick's experience of alien logic actually helps him in his business deals? Business is self-organising chaos, a chaos with its own unique but transitory logic. That logic has to be uncovered, if it is to be managed; maybe a prior exposure to crazy ideas helps?

Not for nothing is alcohol called the 'demon drink.' What I read was the unashamed recollections of a social monster: a self-centred, egotistical, weak-willed and self-deluding demon. However, Brummie Nick was nothing if not brutally honest. He did not try to endear himself to the reader of his diaries. My reaction, which lasted well after finishing his memoirs, was that he deserved a good hiding. His antisocial behaviour, his appalling abuse of, and his taking advantage of, his nearest and dearest, his pathetically inevitable failures when periodically he did manage to jump onto 'the wagon,' were all justified in such a matter-of-fact way that it all seemed perfectly reasonable, almost inevitable. The anecdotes he told were so unreasonably reasonable … described so vividly, and all made perfectly warped sense. Despite myself, I found them very funny, and very moving.

I still find it hard to believe that my ideal neighbour, my exemplar of entrepreneurial management, the now middle-class Nick Charles, is the same person. Brummie Nick was someone else: the stories were the diaries of Mr. Hyde, not kindly Doctor Jekyll. The immediacy in the writing style of the diaries had captured the monster Hyde's twisted logic. I can recommend that anyone who is worried about the effect of drink and drugs on friends or members of their family, or on our society in general, should read these diaries. His book *Through A Glass Brightly*, although lacking the ugly immediacy of the original diaries, still captures his warped thinking and behaviour. See for yourself the appalling damage, sometimes permanent, that alcoholics inflict on themselves, and on those who care for them, as they slide down the slippery slope of alcohol abuse.

But as we have seen, it is not all bad news. For Nick's is also a message of hope, of perseverance, because there is always a way out of the misery and despair, whether these problems are the result of alcoholism or business failure. Nick Charles himself is living proof of that. How does he manage to keep going despite all the unavoidable disasters, few of his own making, that the world keeps throwing at him? It isn't by leaning on metaphorical lamp-posts; but by self-help, self-belief, self-discipline, and not a little help from his friends.

Books and Other Works
by Nick Charles

Through A Glass Brightly
published by Robson / Chrysalis

Nikki... all about secrets
published by Garrick House Ltd.

A Girl Called Ginger
published by Garrick House Ltd.

Lifting The Top Off The Bottle
published by Garrick House Ltd.

Paradise Cost (an audio CD)
published by Garrick House Ltd.

<u>Websites</u>

www.ianangell.com

www.nickcharles.co.uk

www.addictionnetwork.co.uk

www.chaureserv.co.uk

www.alcoholismtreatmentonline.com

www.villapublishing.co.uk